ENDORSEMENTS

In Cindy McGarvie's latest book *Lost Boys,* she artfully draws our attention to a major issue confronting our next generation of young men: the need to develop morally and spiritually resilient young men who have a clear sense of God's purpose for their lives.

By drawing on her own military background and training, Cindy reminds us of the similarities between military preparation and conflict and the nature of the very real spiritual battle in which we are engaged, albeit a battle that is often unseen and too often unrecognised. In many ways, this book is not so much a call to arms as it is a call for the Western church particularly to wake up and seize the opportunity and responsibility we have to become sharers in the shaping of the spiritual life and character of our young men.

I highly recommend this book, particularly to those who are involved in the training, discipleship, and mentoring of our next generation of young men.

Rev. Dr Peter Francis
Principal
Malyon Theological College

As a former school principal and having been involved with young people including youth at risk all my life, I can attest that Cindy McGarvie's book *Lost Boys* is very timely and much needed. Cindy, like myself, has a military background, and her military analogies are very insightful.

Her description of Israel's Defence Force and the defensive strategies it has had to put in place to defend itself is interesting. Israel is surrounded by enemy nations that are bent on its destruction—an intriguing parallel to what young boys in particular are faced with today.

Cindy is right in her estimation. We are involved in a cosmic conflict, a spiritual war against an enemy far more insidious than any of the enemies our country's military has fought against since Federation.

I can recommend Cindy's book *Lost Boys,* with its poignant subtitle of 'Bring them home', because it brings hope in a world where hopelessness prevails.

Barry Rodgers OAM
Australian Light Horse Association

The present dynamics of this post-Christian culture pose huge challenges for young men to walk victoriously in their faith. Cindy identifies and courageously calls out a deadly target aimed squarely at our young men and boys. Her book skillfully articulates the symptoms of a range of issues facing the church and makes a compelling and exciting case for perhaps the most critical element of its cure—the creation of hope for men to rise up and forge forth. This book is one of the most insightful and intelligent books I've read in a long time.

Peter Bain
Chairman
Youth for Christ Australia

Cindy McGarvie is highlighting one of the critical issues of our day, the raising of the next generation and, in particular, our boys, our young men. One of the most important contributions to the health of a society is responsible and purposeful men. Cindy identifies, highlights and encourages us to see the problems facing boys and to do something about it. I recommend this book and trust it engenders much conversation and solutions to build a better society by the way we raise our boys.

Ian Shelton
National Coordinator
Movement Day Australia

This is a fantastic book about a very important subject. We need to look after our boys. Boys become men, and men become fathers. And fathers who turn their hearts toward their children turn the world around.

I think I shall have to steal some of the quotes. Please don't tell anyone!

Warwick Marsh
CEO Dads4Kids

This is a book written by a female CEO who has served in the army and has war in her bones. I love how God has led her to write about Lost Boys as a result of asking hard questions to find some keys to reach the lost men in Australia. She has, I believe, highlighted very specifically the battle that men are being targeted for: to render them impotent as a result of the full-on demonic, unclean assignment of the adversary to take them out permanently through pornography.

When I was given the manuscript, I thought I would be reading it objectively as an issue out there with the lostness of boys and men. I found, though, that there were parts of it where I felt some explanation for me and my identity.

As someone who has been involved in the evangelism and discipleship process of young men and young women over the last thirty-five years, I think the most disappointing, grieving aspect of the ambition I've had, particularly for some young men, is how they have disqualified themselves from the call of God in their lives because of their involvement in pornography. As I think of those young men, I am pleased to say that many of them have been restored and are active in their call. In addition, as I have continued to work with young people mostly in the church, I found that young men who consistently consume porn always plateau in spiritual maturity—they just don't grow; there is a dullness.

There were many standouts in the book, but perhaps the most notable to me personally was that men are made for adventure, the need for a noble cause to fight for. Idleness is the scourge of a destiny-motivated guy who finds the boredom overwhelming.

I'm looking to introduce the book to the staff in Youth with a Mission Perth to help guys particularly understand and deal with the enemy they face every day. Thank you, Cindy.

Peter Brownhill
Perth Director
Youth with a Mission (YWAM)

Lost Boys is not about giving us the answers; it is about challenging our paradigms. It is a brutally honest diagnosis of the health (moral, emotional, and spiritual) of our young men. Chapter 3 is hard going. But keep reading; there is hope. Cindy's direct use of military language and situational analysis is clarifying and thought-provoking. Her work is well researched but annoying, in the best sense of the word. When you have finished reading this book, you will be unsettled and unsatisfied with how you are seeing and communicating with the young men in your life. On the other hand, you will pray for our lost boys more and judge them less. You may also find yourself listening to podcasts and watching YouTubers, whom she quotes. So go for it—read every word, but don't say I didn't warn you!

Dave Brereton
CEO
Youth for Christ International

Cindy McGarvie reminds us of the importance of knowing our enemy in the battlefield world of wokeness, social media, and gender dysphoria. While real guys come in all shapes and temperaments, Cindy calls us to 'man up' in the key area of fathering a generation of Pan-like *Lost Boys,* protecting them from the multi-level threats of porn, feminised faith, and anti-intellectualism. Her remedy? A robust call to adventurous discipleship. As a side point, I found Cindy's last book a goldmine for sermon quotes. This one will be the same, so my prayer is that many people will benefit from her work.

Phil Campbell
Senior Pastor
Mitchelton Presbyterian Church,
Queensland, Australia
Lecturer at Queensland Theological College

LOST BOYS

Bring them home

CINDY MCGARVIE

Lost Boys: Bring them home
Copyright © 2020 by Cindy McGarvie. Updated 2023.

Publisher: YFC Australia, www.yfc.org.au
Youth for Christ Australia is a chartered member nation of Youth for Christ International.

All rights reserved. All Youth for Christ Australia materials, regardless of format, are protected by copyright law. No part may be reproduced and reused for any commercial purpose without written permission from Youth for Christ Australia. For permission requests, write to Youth for Christ Australia via the website or email address info@yfc.org.au

The author asserts her moral rights.

Editing and Typesetting: Sally Hanan at Inksnatcher.com
Cover Design: GermanCreative
Cover Image: PRESSLAB/shutterstock.com

All Scripture references are from the New American Standard Bible® (NASB), unless otherwise noted. Copyright © 1960, 1962, 1963, 1968, 1971, 1972, 1973, 1975, 1977, 1995 by The Lockman Foundation. Used by permission. www.Lockman.org.

Scripture quotations marked (NKJV) are taken from the New King James Version®. Copyright © 1982 by Thomas Nelson. Used by permission. All rights reserved.

Scripture quotations marked (NIV) are taken from the Holy Bible, New International Version®, NIV®. Copyright ©1973, 1978, 1984, 2011 by Biblica, Inc.™ Used by permission of Zondervan. All rights reserved worldwide. www.zondervan.com

A catalogue record for this work is available from the National Library of Australia.

Lost Boys/Bring them home
ISBN 978-0-6483954-1-6
ISBN eBook 978-0-6483954-2-3

This book is dedicated to my three sons, Adin, Josiah, and Eli, once little boys fighting imaginary battles with toy guns and swords, now young men courageously forging forth in life's real adventures and battles.

I'm so proud of you!

CONTENTS

FOREWORD i
PREFACE v

1. PEACE FOR OUR TIME OR NOT? 1
2. THE CENTRE OF GRAVITY 11
3. THE CHANGING CHARACTER OF WAR 25
4. TRAINING SOLDIERS FOR WAR 41
5. WEAPON TRAINING 51
6. FEMINISATION STIFLES MASCULINITY 61
7. ENGAGING THE INTELLECT 75
8. PETER PAN 87
9. COUNTERINSURGENCY 95
10. A NEW BATTLEFRONT 105
11. AND THAT'S HOW IT'S DONE 117
12. GOLIATH'S DEAD 131
A RALLY CALL TO MEN 139

ABOUT THE AUTHOR 141
ACKNOWLEDGEMENTS 143

FOREWORD

How good and timely to have someone write so coherently on the role of men and, particularly, as God intended it—as active and courageous leaders.

As the father of two girls, I am so grateful that my daughters live in a world that encourages women and seeks to create the level playing field in which they can flourish and reach their full potential. That is a necessary correction to long-existing cultural practices that have disadvantaged women.

But it doesn't change the purpose for which God created men. We need to question the motive behind any overcorrection that seeks to weaken that purpose, limit the potential in the inherent difference in men, and recognise it as a spiritual attack striking at the very core of creation, its pinnacle, in God's purpose in creating both man and woman—which He could have done.

Cindy identifies well the analogy of the soldier in encouraging men to step forward to embrace their role in this battle. But more importantly and more uniquely, she uses her own military experience and knowledge to explain how the enemy approaches his destructive task of separating us from God as a battle—a spiritual battle, but no less a battle.

LOST BOYS

The use of battlefield terminology brings into sharp focus the reasons for the prevalent cultural imperative to feminise men and discourage their God-given and naturally evident characteristics of risk-taking and leadership. Placed in Cindy's battlefield context, as one of God's army's strengths, these characteristics of men become something any half-competent opponent would seek to weaken, and he has done it so well. And particularly in the church.

As a student of war with over thirty years of service, I know that the most fundamental error any commander can make is not only to underestimate the enemy but to fail to see the battlefield as it is.

The fact that God was caused to sacrifice his only Son to redeem the world should leave us in no doubt about His assessment of the enemy, about the lengths to which even God saw He had to go to defeat him.

But even if we appreciate the capability of this spiritual enemy, we have certainly shown ourselves to be blinded to the nature of the battlefield. As the church, we continually underestimate the impact of the next cultural change. As often as not, we excuse it, or in the worst case, even support it. Our motives are usually well intended though misplaced. We are too ready to place the cultural mantras of equality and tolerance before truth and fail to see that in compromising truth on issues we are caused to see as peripheral, like gender and marriage, it becomes

Foreword

harder and harder to preserve on the next objective of the enemy. We have allowed him to generate one of his most useful weapons on the battlefield: momentum.

But misreading of the battlefield, if costly, can usually be reversed. History is replete with seemingly hopeless battles turned by leaders with determination and courage. These are not characteristics unique to men; we all know women who display them in full measure. But they are characteristics that God created men to exhibit.

I recommend this book to boys and men as one who identifies the battlefield and calls each of us to step up as men for the sake of the God we serve.

Jim Wallace AM
Brigadier JJA Wallace (Retd.)
Canberra, 2019

PREFACE

I WILL NEVER FORGET THAT EVENING when I came face to face with a young homeless lad who looked exactly like my son. I approached him, and we had a conversation. He had so much potential, but he was homeless, fatherless, destitute, substance-addicted, and lost. That experience left me feeling like my heart had been ripped out of my chest. A question burned in my soul: What if he really were your son, your flesh and blood?

This book came about because I've watched too many young men fall away, rendered impotent due to anxiety and depression, fed lie after lie about their identity and reason for existence, gripped with gender confusion and totally enslaved by addictions such as porn. It's been heart-crushing.

I've listened to too many parents grieving over their lost sons—Lost Boys.

But there are sparks of hope.

Clearly there is freedom and supernatural power in the gospel. Our weapons of warfare are mighty, but our young people need to be taught how to use these weapons. Paul encouraged us that we are 'more than conquerors' and that God 'gives us victory through our Lord Jesus

Christ' (Rom. 8:37; 1 Cor. 15:57). Either this is a lie, or it's not. And if it's not, then victory is indeed ours. I have listened to the stories of young men who have slayed giants with the truth of the gospel. It can be done.

I also want to highlight the movement of young men yearning to find purpose and meaning in their lives and seeking answers. Many of them can be found on social media forums. This is a new public square outside the mainline media dominated by young, incredibly bright thinkers, many of them Christian. Standing alongside these young men you will also find some outstanding father figures. They realise that we are in a battle for the hearts and minds of our young people, and they are on the front lines. What's more, young men are flocking to join them on these front lines of societal revolution.

In many instances, the church needs to catch up. The church needs to know what's happening. More than ever, Christians must awaken and see that we are in a battle and step up into the battlefield.

I trained as an Army nurse and married a soldier, a combat engineer. We have three sons and a son-in-law, all courageous young men. Our eldest son serves as an officer in the Australian Army. The skills and values we learned in the military we still use today. I have an interest in military history and watch perhaps too many war movies and documentaries. I am drawn to chivalry, virtue, honour, and the courage of the men who have fought and still fight for our freedom. I've used the military analogy throughout this book to illuminate the very real battle in which we find ourselves.

So many others have written extensively and more authoritatively on topics I've only briefly touched upon. Perhaps I have given more weight to one issue above another. For instance, fatherlessness is a huge problem that I've only barely covered as a major contributor for the situation of our nation's lost boys. But my hope is that this book will spark in you the desire to take up your weapons of warfare and fight the good fight for our lost boys.

Cindy McGarvie

PEACE FOR OUR TIME OR NOT?

— 1 —

People sleep peaceably in their beds at night only because rough men stand ready to do violence on their behalf.

– George Orwell

IN 1938, BRITISH PRIME MINISTER Neville Chamberlain was greeted by cheers from the crowds as he stepped off the plane after a meeting in Munich with Adolf Hitler, Italian leader Mussolini, and French leader Daladier. The British people still had not yet recovered from World War I, otherwise known as the Great War or *the war to end all wars*. They were nervous about Hitler's military expansionist activities and didn't want to go through the horrors of another war. The British had paid a huge price in the lives of their fathers, brothers, and sons—almost one million men—and there were those who returned maimed and scarred, traumatised to incapacitation. The people were praying, waiting with bated breath, listening by the radio to see if a deal could be struck and war could be avoided.

And the outcome? 'Peace for our time!' Chamberlain announced jubilantly from a second-floor window at 10 Downing Street, his official residence. He added, 'Now I recommend you to go home and sleep quietly in your beds.'[1]

> As Britain slept, the German army marched into Czechoslovakia in "peaceful conquest" of the Sudetenland. The bombers did not roar over London that night, but they would come. In March 1939, Hitler annexed the rest of Czechoslovakia, and two days after the Nazis crossed into Poland on September 1, 1939, the prime minister again spoke to the nation, but this time to solemnly call for a British declaration of war against Germany and the launch of World War II.[2]

Chamberlain was forced to resign eight months after his meeting with Hitler. Winston Churchill, his successor, eventually led the British people to victory after another devastating war. The thing about Churchill was that he saw Hitler for who he truly was when others didn't. He spoke out against Germany's rearmament and about the weakness of the British military in comparison. In 1930, nine years before Britain entered the war, Churchill met with Prince Bismarck at the German Embassy. Even then, the prince noted that Churchill 'was convinced that Hitler or his followers would seize the first available opportunity to resort to armed force'.[3] Churchill had discernment. He understood the times, the evil nature of Hitler, and the reality of the threat.

Peace in our time—we all want that. And in this hyper-safety-conscious day and age, who doesn't?

Now imagine living in a nation where your entire history is comprised of war. At one time your nation existed, then it was gone, then it was back again. Imagine not just sons but daughters required to do national service after leaving school, young men for three years, young women for two.[4] Picture living in hypervigilance with rockets regularly targeted at your homes. That's Israel today, and they are perpetually in a state of war.

Because of this, Israel has one of the most sophisticated military forces in the world. They are a small nation, yet they have 160,000 active frontline military personnel. Their mandatory military service program ensures that a large percentage of the population are militarily ready. In addition, even though other nations' militaries may be large with frontline personnel, tanks, aircraft, warships, and submarines, these only reflect the *quantity* and not *quality* of military forces, such as how well a military is trained and the sophistication of its weapons. Israel has satellites, high-tech armed drones, and nuclear weapons, an extremely sophisticated and effective force.[5] The

LOST BOYS

Israeli Intelligence Community is made up of their military intelligence (Aman), overseas intelligence (Mossad), and internal security (Shabak). Israelis are ranked second in the world in cyber war technology, with some going as far to say Israel leads the world in this.[6]

Just as ancient Israelites in the promised land needed to train up each generation in the art of warfare or else they would be taken captive or annihilated, the Israelis today have mandatory military service because they know all too well they are surrounded not just by people who want to take their land but by people driven by an ideology of hatred toward them. If the Israelis let their guard down for even one minute, a rocket fired from Gaza might just hit its target.

According to the 2018 Israel Defence Forces (IDF) annual report, 1,000 rockets were fired at Israel from Gaza. That averages out to around three per day and is a dramatic increase in number from years prior. That increase led to Israel striking Gaza 865 times in response. Of the 1,000 rockets and mortars fired, 250 were intercepted by Israel's Iron Dome Missile Defence System, which intercepts rockets, artillery, and mortars before they reach their target. The Iron Dome only targets missiles heading toward built-up areas, and some of the missiles get through the system—45 made it through in 2018, and a total of sixteen people were killed.[7]

Because Israel is surrounded by hostile countries—many of whom are fundamentally opposed to Israel's existence as a nation—it has become a leader in defence technology. For example, their Iron Dome Missile Defence System was developed in 2011 and has greatly decreased the carnage from incoming missiles. The US Army announced in 2019 that it intends to buy two Iron Dome batteries to expand its current defence capabilities.[8] More recently, tensions ramped up between Israel and Hamas when in November 2019, 450 rockets were fired out of Gaza at Israel over a thirty-six-hour period. Due to the effectiveness of the Iron Dome defence system, 90 percent of the rockets were intercepted, with only minor injuries and some damage.[9]

All this to say that the nation of Israel—and every single citizen—needs to be battle ready and must be on the cutting edge of defence technology to keep its citizens safe.

Likewise, Christians are in a state of spiritual war.

The Bible is clear that we have been in a cosmic battle since creation between the adversary and God, including mankind, who were created in His image. Every Christian man, woman, and child needs to be trained in spiritual warfare and accustomed to it, or else, like Israel then and now, we face being taken out by our enemy.

> These are the nations the Lord left to test all those Israelites who had not experienced any of the wars in Canaan (he did this only to teach warfare to the

descendants of the Israelites **who had not had previous battle experience**).

> – Judges 3:1-2 NIV (emphasis added)

We have an enemy who wants to destroy us, who is carrying off our children en masse into the captivity of destruction, darkness, and deception. Have we lost the art of spiritual warfare? Are we teaching it to the next generation? Have we forgotten there is an enemy who is on the watch 24/7 to rob, kill, and destroy? Is it that we can only look on helplessly as our sons and daughters are carried off? Charles Kraft wrote, 'Soldiers who are on the battlefield but are not fighting cannot expect to win. This is one reason why so many Christians are living defeated lives'.[10]

The question needs to be asked: Do we have it so good, living in an age of luxury and instant gratification of every kind, that we have become too soft, protective, safety conscious, politically correct, oversensitive, and delicate that we don't want the inconvenience of going out to battle? Are we compromising for peace at all cost?

Matthew Henry (1662–1714), commenting on the Scripture above about the Israelites taking the promised land, brings up this point:

> It appears to have been an act of God's wisdom, that he let them [a remnant of Canaanites] remain for Israel's real advantage, that those who had not known the wars of Canaan might learn war. ... It was the will of God that the people of Israel be inured to war [accustomed to something unpleasant],

1. Because their country was exceedingly rich and fruitful and abounded with dainties of all sorts, which, if they were not sometimes made to know hardship, would be in danger of sinking them into the utmost degree of luxury and effeminacy. They must sometimes wade in blood and not always milk and honey, lest even their men of war, by the long disuse of arms, should become as soft and as nice as the tender and delicate woman, that would not set as much as the sole of her foot to the ground for tenderness and delicacy. ...

2. Because their country lay very much in the midst of enemies, by whom they must expect to be insulted. ... It was therefore necessary they should be well disciplined, that they might defend their coasts when invaded, and might hereafter enlarge their coast as God had promised them. The art of war is best learnt by experience, which not only acquaints men with martial discipline, but (which is no less necessary) inspires them with a martial disposition. It was for the interest of Israel to breed soldiers, as it is the interest of an island to breed sea-men, and therefore God left Canaanites among them that, by the less difficulties and hardships they met with in encountering them, they might be prepared for greater, and, by running with the footmen, might learn to contend with horses Jer. 12:5. Israel was a figure of the church militant, that must fight its way to a triumphant state.[11]

When people live in luxury, it causes them to become weak, delicate, and effeminate.

> Hard times create strong men.
> Strong men create good times.

LOST BOYS

> Good times create weak men.
> And, weak men create hard times.[12]

I believe our good times of prosperity have weakened our society and the church. Many of our sons and daughters have been taken captive or destroyed by the enemy. The devastating stories from parents who have seen what the enemy is capable of doing to their children—confusing them, deceiving them, luring them into addictions and self-destructive habits—are almost too much to bear.

Peace for our time? Hell no, we are at war.

---

[1] Christopher Klein, 'Chamberlain Declares 'Peace for Our Time', 75 Years Ago', *History*, updated August 29, 2018, https://www.history.com/news/chamberlain-declares-peace-for-our-time-75-years-ago.

[2] Klein, 'Peace for Our Time'.

[3] Scott Manning, 'Churchill's Earliest Warning About Hitler', *Historian on the Warpath* (blog), March 8, 2011, https://scottmanning.com/content/churchills-earliest-warning-about-hitler/https://scottmanning.com/content/churchills-earliest-warning-about-hitler.

[4] 'Reality Check: Which countries have military service?', *BBC*, June 28, 2018, https://www.bbc.com/news/world-44646267.

[5] Jeremy Bender, 'RANKED: The world's 20 strongest militaries', *Business Insider*, October 3, 2015, https://www.businessinsider.com/these-are-the-worlds-20-strongest-militaries-ranked-2015-9?r=AU&IR=T#14-israel-7.

[6] Bob Mason, 'So Who Has the Most Advanced Cyber Warfare Technology?', *FX Empire*, accessed November 9, 2019, https://www.fxempire.com/education/article/so-who-has-the-most-advanced-cyber-warfare-technology-444874.

[7] Anna Ahronheim, 'IDF annual report: 1,000 rockets fired at Israel from Gaza in 2018', *Jerusalem Post*, December 31, 2018, https://www.jpost.com/Arab-Israeli-Conflict/IDF-1000-rockets-fired-at-southern-Israel-from-Gaza-over-the-past-year-575871.

[8] 'Iron Dome and Skyhunter Systems: Short-Range Air Defense', *Raytheon*, accessed September 7, 2019, https://www.raytheon.com/capabilities/products/irondome.

[9] Haaretz, 'Israel Strikes Islamic Jihad Positions Following Rockets Launched From Gaza After Ceasefire', Haaretz, Nov 15, 2019, https://www.haaretz.com/israel-news/islamic-jihad-israel-gaza-rockets-ceasefire-tel-aviv-hamas-syria-1.8122258.

[10] Charles H. Kraft, *I Give You Authority: Practicing the Authority Jesus Gave Us*, (Bloomington, MN: Baker Publishing Group, 2012), 34.

[11] Matthew Henry, *Bible Commentary,* s.v. 'Judges 3,' accessed November 19, 2019, https://www.christianity.com/bible/commentary.php?com=mh&b=7&c=3.

[12] G. Michael Hopf, *Those Who Remain* (self-pub., 2016), Kindle.

THE CENTRE OF GRAVITY

— 2 —

The talent of the strategist is to identify the decisive point and to concentrate everything on it.

— Carl von Clausewitz, *On War*

ON THE 27TH OF FEBRUARY, 1991, US armed forces clashed with the Iraqi forces in what has gone down on record as one of the largest tank battles in US history. It was the Battle of Medina Ridge in Operation Desert Storm. The US forces not just defeated the Republican Guard, the elite branch of Saddam Hussein's military, in a mere 40 minutes, they *pulverised* them.[1] In that short time, they destroyed 186 tanks and 127 armoured vehicles.[2] Few Iraqis survived the battle. Most were incinerated in their vehicles. When the American forces first met with the Iraqi forces before the battle, the Iraqi tanks and military posture were facing another direction and were caught unawares. The Americans lost one soldier from 'friendly fire' and four tanks. The US M1 Abrams tanks were far superior to the outdated Russian made T-72 and outmoded Chinese Type 69 tanks. The American tanks were not only faster, they fired from distances around 2,500 metres on the move, which was well outside the range of the inferior Iraqi tanks, which had to be stationary to fire and with a range of up to 1,700 metres.

> "It was brief, it was intense and it was one-sided," said Doug Woolley, a retired Army lieutenant colonel who led a platoon in the battle.
>
> And it was one of the final punches of Gen. Norman Schwarzkopf's "left hook" — a massive flanking attack against Iraqi forces near the Kuwait border. The tank crews of 1st Armored Division had moved at a blistering pace through southern Iraq since crossing the Saudi border three days earlier, meeting little resistance along the way.[3]

This battle was decisive. An Iraqi cease-fire went into effect the following day, and the Americans began withdrawing and were home a few weeks later.

A Prussian general named Carl von Clausewitz wrote a book called *On War*, one of the greatest works on military strategy and theory in history. In his writings he explains about the 'centre of gravity'. Centres of gravity are 'the source of power' for both friendly and enemy forces.[4] When military commanders strategise for battle, they

The Centre of Gravity

focus on taking out these centres of gravity to disempower their enemy and gain victory. Centres of gravity can be physical, which consist of the operational capabilities, or they can be moral centres of gravity, which pertain to the will of the people to fight and the ability of the leaders and others of influence on both sides.[5]

In the Persian Gulf War at the Battle of Medina Ridge, the Iraqi operational centre of gravity was targeted. The elite Republican Guard, the most powerful of Iraq's forces, was destroyed, and the war was won. At that point, the moral centre of gravity, Saddam Hussein, remained undefeated as the US forces were not given permission by the UN to enter Baghdad. Hussein was finally taken out in 2003 in Operation Iraqi Freedom, and the regime was toppled.[6] Obviously, the unrest in the Middle East, with the Arab Spring and ISIS, and the hostility toward Israel and the West is much bigger than Saddam Hussein, and thus, it continues. However, the Battle of Medina Ridge is a good example for explaining the operational centre of gravity for our purposes here.

If a clandestine enemy wanted to attack a nation of people scattered throughout the world (Christians) to cripple them spiritually and prevent their flourishing, what would be the centre of gravity to target heavily? I believe it would be the men, particularly the young, vibrant, fighting-age men.

LOST BOYS

Neutralise men and get them at the youngest possible age when they are weak and vulnerable. By the time they reach fighting age, they will have no strength and no will to fight. Neither will they have any idea of their potential, their purpose or who they really are.

There is something incredible about boys growing up to be strong men who forge, conquer, invent, build, and take valiant risks. Brave men who fight for our freedoms in horrendous wars, who provide and protect and serve, who learn to lead with integrity and boldly stand for righteousness. God created mankind in His image, and a man living to his God-given potential is a powerful force to be reckoned with.

Indeed I believe the enemy's chief strategy to take out men is to go after the easiest target—the young ones, our boys—and I aim to prove this point.

Let's look at the evidence.

THE SUICIDE CRISIS

Across the world there is a male suicide crisis.

In Australia, suicide is the biggest killer of young people aged twelve to twenty-four, and this is steadily on the increase. Suicide is the leading cause of death in males from ages fifteen to forty-four. In 2017, 2,348 men and boys died by suicide, an increase of 10 percent from the previous year. That averages out to forty-five male deaths per week. In 2017, the number of boys under fifteen years who took their own life increased by an astounding 77 percent. In addition to this, there is a level of underreporting that may distort youth suicide data both in Australia and worldwide.[7]

An Australian Parliamentary post for the 2019 International Men's Week reports on men's mental health:

> In a 12 month period, from July 2015 to June 2016, there were 112,637 ambulance attendances for men experiencing acute mental health issues. ... The report provides further detail on self-harm related attendances, stating there were 30,197 in the 12 month period (306 male per 100,000), including self-injury, self-injury ideation (or threat), suicidal ideation (thoughts), suicide attempt and suicides, and almost all of these cases were transported to hospital. There were almost twice as many ambulance attendances for suicidal ideation than attempts, but both often involved police. Overdose was the most common way for men to attempt suicide. For almost half of suicidal ideation related attendances, the male involved had a clear suicide plan.[8]

And it's not just Australia. This trend of male suicide, particularly in young men, is happening around the globe. The UK has declared a 'male suicide crisis',[9] with one researcher claiming more men in the UK dying from suicide in the past year 'than all British soldiers fighting in all wars since 1945'.[10] I actually looked up how many wars the British have fought since 1945, and there are scores of them, from Vietnam to the Kenyan Mau Mau Uprising to the Malaya Emergency, just to name a few.

LOST BOYS

According to my own research, in 2018, 4,903 UK men died at their own hands,[11] and 7,185 British soldiers have died in operational deaths between 1945 and 2016. So the figures are more equivalent to more UK men dying by suicide in 2018 and 2019 than British soldiers *in all wars* since 1945,[12] but that's still a significant number.

In the US there has been a 100 percent increase in suicide rates of kids 10 to 14 years old.[13] Warren Farrell, coauthor of *The Boy Crisis: Why Our Boys Are Struggling and What We Can Do About It*, contributing on America's suicide problem states, 'It is a crisis of mental health. Boys' suicide rate goes from only slightly more than girls before age 15 to three times that of girls' between 15 and 19, to 4 1/2 times that of girls between 20 and 24'.[14]

Randolph Nesse, Director of the Arizona State University Center for Evolution and Medicine, claims that 'being male is now the single largest demographic factor for early death'.[15]

And the thief comes only to steal, kill, and destroy (John 10:10).

FATHERLESSNESS

Ample research suggests that the current suicide epidemic we are facing across the globe is heavily linked to the current fatherlessness crisis we are facing as well.

Fatherlessness is taking its toll on our boys. According to the USA website Fathers.com, 'An estimated 24.7 million children (33%) live absent their biological father'.[16] That's one in three children in America growing up fatherless, or what may be termed *orphaned*. One study puts it down to '40% of all boys live in a fatherless home due to divorce, separation, and absentee dads just working full time. America leads the industrialised world in this domain of fatherless families'.[17] In biblical patriarchal times, a child without a father was considered an orphan.[18]

The orphan spirit is rife.

And while this fatherlessness affects girls as well, the negative consequences for boys are astounding. Boys are impacted by fatherlessness significantly more than girls. The average IQ of boys in the UK has dropped a whopping 15 points since the 1980s, and one of a number of contributing factors is less time spent with fathers. One study indicated that time spent with a father prior to age eleven increases a child's IQ.[19]

Fatherless children are the most vulnerable and powerless in our society. Compared to their peers living with both of their biological parents, children raised in single-parent homes have a:

> 77 percent greater risk of being physically abused;
>
> 87 percent greater risk of being harmed by physical neglect;
>
> 165 percent greater risk of experiencing notable physical neglect;

74 percent greater risk of suffering from emotional neglect;

80 percent greater risk of suffering serious injury as a result of abuse;

120 percent greater risk of experiencing some type of maltreatment overall.[20]

Scores of books have already been written on fatherlessness and its devastating effects. The aforementioned book, released in 2018 and titled *The Boy Crisis: Why Our Boys Are Struggling and What We Can Do About It*, contains some excellent research. One of the authors, Warren Farrell, was featured in a *Washington Times* article stating, 'The frequency at which fathers are absent has been devastating for the development of boys.' Farrell 'pointed to research showing that boys without fathers fare worse than boys with fathers on more than 70 different metrics.' He went on to say, 'They're much more likely to drink, much more likely to do drugs, much more likely to be depressed, much more likely to be suicidal, much more likely to be violent, much more likely to be in prison … and they're also much more likely to commit mass shootings.'[21]

And fatherless boys beget fatherless boys.

The effects of such fatherlessness couldn't be clearer than what is seen in the black communities of America. In the US, 'more black boys between ten and twenty years are killed by homicides than by the next nine leading causes of death combined'.[22] The African American boy crisis is that they are either committing murder or being murdered. The fatherless ratio is significantly higher in these communities, almost doubling that of white children.[23]

In his book *Why Young Men: The Dangerous Allure of Violent Movements and What We Can do About It*, Jamil Jivani provides some interesting research and insights on young men. He writes about how young black men growing up without fathers often find their identity and a sense of community in gangs that foster anti-social and criminal behavior.[24] In the US, there has been a 700 percent increase in the prison population over the forty-one years from 1972–2013, with 93 percent being both male and disproportionately young.[25]

TOXIC FEMINISM

Lastly, it would be remiss of me to not include the undermining attack on men through the feminist movement, which started heading in the wrong direction in the 1960s. Our sons are bearing the weight of this. Many, including myself, call this *toxic feminism*.[26] Mallory Millett, sister of Kate Millett, a major influencer in the Women's Liberation Movement and who wrote the book *Sexual Politics*, spoke out against her sister and her destructive philosophy based on Marxist ideology. *Time Magazine* called Kate "'the Karl Marx of the Women's

Movement" ... because her book laid out a course in Marxism 101 for women'.[27]

In 1969 Mallory joined Kate's 'consciousness-raising-group' a number of times and witnessed with disbelief the 'litany' when the chairperson would open the meetings:

> "Why are we here today?" she asked.
> "To make revolution," they answered.
> "What kind of revolution?" she replied.
> "The Cultural Revolution," they chanted.
> "And how do we make Cultural Revolution?" she demanded.
> "By destroying the American family!" they answered.
> "How do we destroy the family?" she came back.
> "By destroying the American Patriarch," they cried exuberantly.
> "And how do we destroy the American Patriarch?" she replied.
> "By taking away his power!"
> "How do we do that?"
> "By destroying monogamy!" they shouted.
> "How can we destroy monogamy?"...
> "By promoting promiscuity, eroticism, prostitution and homosexuality!" they resounded.[28]

That was 1969, more than fifty years ago. Hence, the gradual undermining of the family, the basic building block of healthy societies.

Kate Millett's writings 'captivated the academic classes and soon "Women's Studies" courses were installed in colleges in a steady wave ... with Kate Millett books as required reading.... The goal of Women's Liberation is to wear each female down to losing all empathy for boys, men or babies'.[29]

One of the teachings of this radical ideology was that marriage is a form of slavery and forced prostitution and must be destroyed. It was not so long ago that Australia had a female prime minister, a strong feminist who was once president of the Australian Union of Students (AUS). The AUS adopted a policy on prostitution, 'Prostitution takes many forms and is not only the exchange of money for sex ... [but] prostitution in marriage is the transaction of sex in return for love, security and housekeeping',[30] an idea taken right out of Kate Millett's book.

Christina Hoff Somers, an academic known for her critique of contemporary feminism, warned, 'Moms and dads, be afraid for your sons. There's a "war on men" that started a long time ago in gender studies classes and in women's advocacy groups eager to believe that men are toxic. ... Many educated women in the U.S have drunk from the gender feminist Kool Aid. ... [They] see themselves as oppressed. This is madness'.[31]

Our ABC national broadcaster aired their Monday night Q&A program early in November 2019 with a group of six feminists who freely exposed their radical views, advocating violence and sprinkled with comments such as 'F*** the patriarchy'.[32] It was painful to watch as they appeared as angry, bitter women who purported to advocate for women's rights. The audience was given a good glimpse of the hostile and unpleasant fruit of the feminist ideology. Interestingly, after significant complaints, ABC removed the show from iView and launched an investigation.

The contemporary feminist movement was way ahead with their social engineering agenda. They have focused intensely on men as the centre of gravity and have aimed to destroy the patriarchy, thereby dismantling traditional family structures. The fallout has been devastating.

It's no wonder that when the pharaoh of Egypt saw the potential of the Israelites, he clearly recognised the centre of gravity and ordered the baby boys to be killed at birth. Then he subjugated the rest into slavery, making them impotent, ineffectual, and powerless.

A battle is ensuing. Our boys and men are being targeted because they are the centre of gravity. Take out our men, and families are weakened and women and children are vulnerable. Our men are being subdued without even a fight.

---

[1] Steven Beardsley, 'Largest US tank battle lasted mere minutes', Stars and Stripes, accessed November 19, 2019, https://www.stripes.com/news/special-reports/the-gulf-war-25-year-anniversary/medina-ridge.
[2] 'Battle of Medina Ridge', Military Wikia.org, accessed November 19, 2019, https://military.wikia.org/wiki/Battle_of_Medina_Ridge.
[3] Steven Beardsley, 'Largest US tank battle'.
[4] Robert Dixon, 'Clausewitz, Center of Gravity, and the Confusion of a Generation of Planners', *Small Wars Journal*, accessed November 19, 2019, https://smallwarsjournal.com/jrnl/art/clausewitz-center-of-gravity-and-the-confusion-of-a-generation-of-planners.

[5] Joseph L. Strange and Richard Iron, 'Center of Gravity: What Clausewitz Really Meant', *JFQ Forum*, accessed November 19, 2019, https://apps.dtic.mil/dtic/tr/fulltext/u2/a520980.pdf.

[6] Strange and Iron, 'Center of Gravity'.

[7] 'Young people', Life in Mind, accessed November 19, 2019, https://www.lifeinmindaustralia.com.au/about-suicide/suicide-across-the-lifespan/young-people.

[8] Joanne Simon-Davies, 'International Men's Health Week', Parliament of Australia, June 14, 2019, https://www.aph.gov.au/About_Parliament/Parliamentary_Departments/Parliamentary_Library/FlagPost/2019/June/Mens_health.

[9] Sam Parker, 'What can we do about Britain's male suicide crisis?', *Esquire*, May 9, 2017, https://www.esquire.com/uk/culture/a9202/britain-male-suicide-crisis.

[10] Warren Farrell, PhD and John Gray, PhD, *The Boy Crisis: Why Our Boys are Struggling and What We Can Do about It* (Dallas: BenBella Books Inc, 2018), 34.

[11] 'Suicides in the UK: 2018 registrations', Office for National Statistics, accessed November 19, 2019, https://www.ons.gov.uk/peoplepopulationandcommunity/birthsdeathsandmarriages/deaths/bulletins/suicidesintheunitedkingdom/2018registrations.

[12] 'UK Armed Forces Deaths: Operational deaths post World War II', Ministry of Defence, March 31, 2016, https://assets.publishing.service.gov.uk/government/uploads/system/uploads/attachment_data/file/512070/20160331_UK_Armed_Forces_Operational_deaths_post_World_War_II.O.pdf.

[13] 'QuickStats: Death Rates for Motor Vehicle Traffic Injury, Suicide, and Homicide Among Children and Adolescents aged 10–14 Years — United States, 1999–2014', Morbidity and Mortality Weekly Report (MMWR): Centers for Disease Control and Prevention (CDC), November 4, 2016, http://dx.doi.org/10.15585/mmwr.mm6543a8.

[14] Warren Farrell, 'Boy Crisis' threatens America's future with economic, health and suicide risks', *USA Today*, April 7, 2019, https://www.usatoday.com/story/opinion/2019/04/07/males-risk-boy-crisis-identity-america-future-addiction-suicide-column/3331366002.

[15] Farrell and Gray, *The Boy Crisis*, 20.

[16] 'The Extent of Fatherlessness', Fathers.com, accessed November 19, 2019, http://fathers.com/statistics-and-research/the-extent-of-fatherlessness.

[17] Rosemary K.M. Sword and Philip Zimbardo PhD, 'The Fatherless Generation: What's causing the emotional vacancy in our boys?', *Psychology Today*, August 6, 2018, https://www.psychologytoday.com/au/blog/the-time-cure/201808/the-fatherless-generation.

[18] J.T. Fitzgerald, 'Orphans in Mediterranean Antiquity and Early Christianity', 2016, accessed September 23, 2019, http://www.scielo.org.za/pdf/at/v36s23/03.pdf.

[19] Farrell and Gray, *The Boy Crisis*, 35.

[20] Jill Goldman and Marsha K. Salus with Deborah Wolcott and Kristie Y. Kennedy, 'A Coordinated Response to Child Abuse and Neglect: The Foundation for Practice', U.S. Department of Health and Human Services, 2003, https://www.childwelfare.gov/pubPDFs/foundation.pdf, 31.

[21] Bradford Richardson, 'Link between mass shooters, absent fathers ignored by anti-gun activists', *The Washington Times*, March 27, 2018, https://www.washingtontimes.com/news/2018/mar/27/mass-shooters-absent-fathers-link-ignored-anti-gun.

[22] Farrell and Gray, *The Boy Crisis*, 16.

[23] Zenitha Prince, 'Census Bureau: Higher Percentage of Black Children Live with Single Mothers', *The AFRO.com,* December 31, 2016, https://www.afro.com/census-bureau-higher-percentage-black-children-live-single-mothers.

[24] Jamil Jivani, *Why Young Men: The Dangerous Allure of Violent Movements and What We Can Do About It* (New York: All Points, 2019), 19.

[25] Farrell and Gray, *The Boy Crisis*, 17.

[26] An anti-male attitude that views all men as violent and sexist

[27] Mallory Millett, 'Marxist Feminism's Ruined Lives: The horror I witnessed inside the women's "liberation' movement"', *Frontpage Mag*, September 1, 2014, https://archives.frontpagemag.com/fpm/marxist-feminisms-ruined-lives-mallory-millett.

[28] Millett, 'Marxist Feminism's Ruined Lives',

[29] Ibid.

[30] Tim Andrews, 'Julia Gillard downplays her radical past', Menzies House, August 5, 2010, http://www.menzieshouse.com.au/julia-gillard-downplays-her-radical-past.

[31] Millett, 'Marxist Feminism's Ruined Lives'.

[32] Amanda Meade, 'ABC pulls Q&A's "confronting" feminist debate from iView amid investigation', *The Guardian,* November 8, 2019, https://www.theguardian.com/media/2019/nov/08/abc-pulls-qas-confronting-feminist-debate-from-iview-amid-investigation.

The Changing Character of War

Cyber Warfare

− 3 −

Be extremely subtle even to the point of formlessness. Be extremely mysterious even to the point of soundlessness. Thereby you can be the director of the opponent's fate.

— Sun Tzu, *The Art of War*

THIS IS A WARNING. What you are about to read in this chapter is confronting. It may leave you with a sense of overwhelming despair. One young man who read it told me that he felt like he was being punched over and over again. I looked at condensing the chapter further; however, I believe that the information contained is extremely important for Christians to know. I urge you to bear with me, as the chapters after this one will provide some interesting insight and encouragement. Knowledge is power.

Let's begin.

According to news reports, on June 30th, 2019, an American Global Hawk drone, an unmanned aerial vehicle, was shot down by an Iranian surface-to-air missile. The Iranians accused the US of entering their airspace.[1] The American government reacted to this incident by threatening a retaliatory strike against Iran. However, they pulled back moments before, and instead approved an offensive cyber strike that disabled the computer database used by Iran's Islamic Revolutionary Guard Corps to plan attacks on oil tankers.

> 'Though crippling to Iran's military command and control systems,' reported the Washington Post, 'the operation did not involve a loss of life or civilian casualties—a contrast to conventional strikes, which the president said he called back Thursday because they would not be "proportionate"'.[2]

An attack without involving soldiers or guns, or even leaving the shores of their nation, but crippling nevertheless. The US could have ordered airstrikes on Iran's military bases, where the missiles were launched, but instead they used both *soundless and formless* computer technology to achieve a similar end. This is cyber warfare.

Cyber warfare is 'the use of computer technology to disrupt activities of a state or organization'.[3] It's effective and powerful, as 'the information domain has become the centre of gravity in Clausewitzian terms – the source of power that provides an actor with moral or physical strength'.[4]

Our society today is changing more rapidly than during the industrial revolution.[5] Most of our lives are spent on cyber devices for work, schedules and calendars, communication, education and research, banking, social media, news, entertainment, government departments, health, retail, gas and electricity, and the list goes on and on. Cyber is ubiquitous, or the closest humans can get to omnipresence. Therefore, it has the capacity to do great good or indescribable malice.

Cyber warfare can be used to change society, perhaps even to bring down a democracy by spreading information that makes people lose trust in their government. It can be used to influence culture and can affect the trust, identity, and speech of the people.[6] Our cognitive space can be manipulated right in the privacy of our own homes at any time of the day through internet devices. War can be waged in cyberspace without ever firing a shot.[7]

Pornography

Our adversary has been using cyber warfare for decades. I believe one of his deadliest strategies is pornography. Its reach has been pervasive on men—old and young, married and single, fathers, grandfathers, brothers, sons, and even our little boys. It has even reached our girls. Every debauched, perverted, and vulgar sexual act one can imagine from any pit of darkness around the world is now accessible, affordable, anonymous, and aggressive toward little children.[8] Kids are watching it on their phones in the playground and are consuming porn sometimes multiple times per day, as you'll read in some of the young men's personal accounts later in this book. And this has been happening for years right under our noses.

Consider this. Telstra researched smartphone use and found that 68 percent of children aged three to seventeen in Australia have one, and the average time spent each week on them is twenty-one hours and forty-eight minutes.[9] And this doesn't include computer and tablet use.

Sadly, kids with unrestricted and unsupervised use of devices is having detrimental effects. Research by a security technology company found that 'one in 10 visitors of porn sites is under 10 years old'.[10] Children are not just viewing what we would imagine as normal porn, they are consuming some of the most degrading and violent scenes imaginable, even live-streamed.

Porn is said to be more addictive than heroin, Dr. Jeffrey Satinover wrote:

> With the advent of the computer [and smartphone], the delivery system for this addictive stimulus [internet pornography] has become nearly resistance-free.

> It is as though we have devised a form of heroin 100 times more powerful than before, usable in the privacy of one's own home and injected directly to the brain through the eyes. It's now available in unlimited supply via a self-replicating distribution network, glorified as art and protected by the Constitution.[11]

According to Fight the New Drug, the UK has had a 400-percent increase in child-on-child sexual assaults:

> In a report by The Daily Mail, convictions of rape by those aged under 17 years old have almost doubled in just four years in the UK. A representative from the country's Ministry of Justice has warned that extreme pornography is fueling this alarming rise in the number of child rapists. Experts say violent pornography is influencing children to act out the aggressive, hardcore scenes they see online.[12]

This is not just a problem in the UK. Sexual Assault Nurse Examiner (SANE) Heidi Olson, from the US, writes:

> The biggest age range of perpetrators that I see in my hospital is CHILDREN. In fact, in 2016, 2017, and continuing this year in 2018, our biggest age range of people committing sexual assaults are children ages 11-15 years old. ... Pornography is often a driving factor, and sometimes the only factor that influenced a child to act out in a sexually harmful way. As I have studied our data, and seen more and more patients, it's imperative that we understand the way that pornography is creating devastating effects for children across our country.[13]

LOST BOYS

Kids have become the unwitting 'pushers' of porn, targeting their classmates by either introducing them to porn or playing it out on others. Little kids can go where adult predators can't.

And there's another phenomenon, probably a by-product of consuming porn:

> A study from Northwestern University analyzed comments posted on MTV's website A Thin Line - a site aimed at preventing online sexual abuse.
>
> Of the 462 comments examined, two-thirds of the girls aged 12 to 18 said they had been asked by a boy to send nude photos
>
> A majority reported being pressured, threatened or harassed by boys if they did not comply and only 12 cases reported no backlash for saying 'no'.[14]

These findings cause me to rethink the protections state governments provide for our children with the Working with Children Check. What protections might there need to be in the future to prevent sexual abuse of our children by other children who have free, unrestricted access?

> A 2007 review of research on the matter by Jill Manning demonstrated that children exposed to pornography may become obsessed with acting out adult sexual acts that they have seen; and children under 12 years old who have viewed pornography are statistically more likely to sexually assault their peers. ... Professor Freda Briggs (now deceased), foundation chair of child development at the University of South Australia, in a submission to the 2016 Senate

Inquiry into Harm Being Done to Australian Children through Access to Pornography on the Internet, maintained that child sex offenders used pornography to seduce targeted victims:

> 'There is international evidence that some children become addicted to downloading pornography and rape younger children ... clearly we are paying too high a price for adults' right to view whatever they wish regardless of the consequences for young people and society.'[15]

Depression is a raging epidemic in men and boys and also a side effect of consuming porn.[16] "'Any time [a person] spends much time with the usual pornography usage cycle, it can't help but be a depressing, demeaning, self-loathing kind of experience," says Dr. Gary Brooks, a psychologist who has worked with porn addicts for the last 30 years'.[17] After researching this chapter, it was easy to see the correlation between the increase in porn use in boys and the increase in suicide. We are indeed in a health crisis.

What about marriage and relationships? According to *Psychology Today*, consuming porn harms intimacy and healthy connections. Porn-free relationships are stronger and more committed. The fantasy alternative of porn leads to real-life cheating.[18]

Research undertaken on the impact of porn on marriage breakdown gives evidence to its detrimental effects. Here's just one of many findings:

LOST BOYS

> The American Academy of Matrimonial Lawyers stated that "obsessive interest in pornographic sites" was cited as a major reason for divorce in 56 per cent of cases, second only to "met new love interest over the internet", at 68 per cent. This makes a lie of the oft-heard claim by pornography advocates that pornography helps spice up marriages in peril of breakdown due to boredom.[19]

Dr. James Weaver says, 'In men, prolonged exposure to pornography creates and enhances sexual callousness toward women ... [resulting] in both a loss of respect for female sexual autonomy and the disinhibition of men in the expression of aggression against women.'[20]

At a march against violence toward women in Brisbane, YouTuber 'Krocs On' interviewed women of all ages to get their opinions. One question she asked was, 'Where do men get their violence?' In other words, who's telling men to rape or be violent toward women, as it's not socially acceptable? The answers were very interesting. Some said it was society, some said other men or toxic masculinity (treating women less equal to men and thinking of them as objects sexually). One woman said, 'I don't know. If I knew that, it would be a hell of a lot easier to solve it.'[21]

Let me suggest a cause that many researchers have already concluded: Porn consumption is feeding the escalation of violence toward women, particularly by those who start at a young age. This, I believe, is one of the causes, if not the *major* cause of, toxic masculinity—treating women with callousness and seeing them as sexual objects. I am perplexed as to why this issue should not be on the absolute top of the current feminist agenda. But alas, many modern-day feminists in Australia are missing in action or, worse, defending vocations of the porn industry and sex work as legitimate and harmless job choices for women that can be regulated by the government.

Politicians and women advocates fighting for the legalisation of prostitution believing it liberates women are on another planet.

OUR CURRENT SEXUAL CULTURE

Recently, I watched *The Candice Owens Show* when she interviewed Michael Knowles. Both Candace and Michael are Millennials, or Gen Ys, and two of the brightest social and political commentators of their generation. They are also both Christians. They were discussing some of the issues faced by young people today, when Michael made the comment that Millennials are having less sex compared to previous generations.[22] In this oversexualised culture, how could this be true? I had to go look it up, and I found that he's right: according to my research, Millennials are having less sex than generations before, and it's generated a lot of discussion on reasons for this.[23] However, Michael went on to say that, in his opinion, it's due to the 'masturbatory culture' of consuming porn.[24]

LOST BOYS

I came across several researchers warning of the side effects of porn consumption. This article in the Italian ANSA, or the Italian national press agency, stating that Italy's men are suffering 'sexual anorexia' due to internet porn use, sums them up very well:

> More and more young Italian men are suffering from 'sexual anorexia' and are unable to get erections because of Internet porn use that started in their mid-teens, experts have said. A survey of 28,000 users found that many Italian males started an 'excessive consumption' of porn sites as early as 14 and after daily use in their early to mid-20s became inured to 'even the most violent' images, said Carlo Foresta, head of the Italian Society of Andrology and Sexual Medicine (SIAMS). After developing their sexuality largely divorced from real-life relationships, Foresta said, the effects were gradual but devastating.[25]

Michael Knowles goes on the say in his interview that consuming porn causes a person to 'stop thinking', which makes them 'vulnerable to be overpowered'.[26]

With the young men I've interviewed while researching this book, two themes kept coming through: porn has messed with their identity, and porn can confuse sexual orientation when viewed as a child. If boys (and girls) are exposed to gay porn, whether accidentally or through curiosity, and this produces an involuntary physiological arousal, then a young person may believe this is evidence that they must be gay or bisexual.

This is illustrated well in a powerful video called 'Hudson's Story'.[27] Hudson shares about his experience with gay porn as a teen and his sexual abuse. He remembers when he believed the lie that 'this is who I am' and, as a result, lost the hope of ever becoming a husband or a father, 'the one joy which he was forever barred'.[28] This, of course, led him to a dark place of depression. 'The world was trying to get me to say, "This is who I am, this is my identity." ... All on account of the attractions that I never chose to experience.'[29]

In a recent conversation with a young gay man, he shared with me that he came to the realization he was gay when he was thirteen years old after watching gay porn. I asked him why he watched it in the first place. He said he was just a curious kid, like most.

Internet porn has been a hot topic for discussion on social media due to the shocking number of child consumers. An interesting conversation on the YouTube channel Slightly Offens*ve had some young social commentators discussing the issue.[30] They brought up the point that on what is probably the largest porn site on the internet, one of the top five search suggestions presented had gay sex at number one. Given the small gay population worldwide, it would be hard to believe that gay sex would be ranked the most popular visited category on the site. They concluded that it could be argued that this site is actively promoting the gay sex experience, pushing the perception that it is extremely popular.

Research done by a porn site regarding digital sexuality concludes that 'watching too much porn ... might make you bi'.[31] A young gay man, Matt Bernstein, who has described himself on social media as 'NYC proud fairy, beauty but make it political, he/him', has over one million followers across the globe. He has previously answered questions from his subscribers, and one question stands out:

> Q: when or how did u know u were gay/bi/trans/queer etc?
>
> A: I've known since I was about 10, but was proven once I learned about porn
>
> Q: I don't mean this as a joke —at all—there is something to be said for how many of us learned we were gay via porn and what that potentially means for the importance of access to porn? hmm[32]

Hmm indeed. The enemy's strategy to sexualise and pornify this generation, cripple them with shame, guilt, and depression, cause them to lose their God-given identities, and neutralise the power of men through this type of cyber warfare is nothing less than brilliant. It has rendered our men—the protectors of families and communities—impotent mentally, physically, and spiritually and given rise to toxic masculinity.

And women and children suffer.

The Changing Character of War

And the church is not without its casualties.

Thus, said the great war general and military strategist Sun Tzu, 'The supreme art of war is to subdue the enemy without fighting.'

---

[1] Lily Hay Newman, 'The Drone Iran Shot Down Was a $220M Surveillance Monster', *Wired,* June 20, 2019, https://www.wired.com/story/iran-global-hawk-drone-surveillance.

[2] Zak Doffman, 'U.S Attacks Iran with Cyber Not Missiles—A Game Changer, Not A Backtrack', *Forbes,* June 23, 2019, https://www.forbes.com/sites/zakdoffman/2019/06/23/u-s-attacks-iran-with-cyber-not-missiles-a-game-changer-not-a-backtrack/#4cde939753fa.

[3] Bob Mason, 'So Who Has the Most Advanced Cyber Warfare Technology?', FX Empire, accessed November 9, 2019, https://www.fxempire.com/education/article/so-who-has-the-most-advanced-cyber-warfare-technology-444874.

[4] Zachery Tyson Brown, 'Unmasking War's Changing Character', Modern War Institute at West Point, March 12, 2019, https://mwi.usma.edu/unmasking-wars-changing-character.

[5] Becky Sweat, 'How Can We Cope in a World of Rapid Change?', Beyond Today, August 1, 2010, https://www.ucg.org/the-good-news/how-can-we-cope-in-a-world-of-rapid-change.

[6] Defense One Staff, 'Ep. 48: Cyberwarfare today', Defense One, July 12, 2019, https://www.defenseone.com/ideas/2019/07/ep-48-cyberwarfare-today/158387.

[7] Brown, 'Unmasking War's Changing Character'.

[8] Charles D. Knutson, 'The Four A's of Internet Pornography', in Digital Mists of Darkness, accessed November 25, 2019, http://digitalmists.com/read/chapter-4/the-four-as.

[9] Chris McCormack, 'Society: The pervasive and pernicious online porn epidemic', *NewsWeekly,* April 6, 2019, http://www.newsweekly.com.au/article.php?id=58479.

[10] Răzvan Muresan, 'One in 10 visitors of porn sites is under 10 years old', Hot for Security: Bitdefender, September 20, 2016, https://hotforsecurity.bitdefender.com/blog/one-in-10-visitors-of-porn-sites-is-under-10-years-old-16675.html.

[11] Jeffrey Satinover, M.S., M.D., 'Jeffrey Satinover Statement to Congress on Pornography', May 9, 2008, https://www.scribd.com/document/44914401/Jeffrey-Satinover.

LOST BOYS

[12] 'How Violent Porn Fueled A 400% Rise in Child-On-Child Assaults in the UK', Fight the New Drug, August 22, 2019, https://fightthenewdrug.org/how-porn-fuels-child-on-child-sex-attacks.

[13] 'What Porn and Shame Have to do with Child-On-Child Sexual Assault', *Fight the New* Drug, April 5, 2019, https://fightthenewdrug.org/heidi-olson-sane-child-on-child-sexual-assault-and-porn.

[14] Kayla Brantley, 'Teenage girls describe the brutal pressure from boys to text nude photos – and the threats and harassment if they refuse', *Daily Mail*, January 4, 2018, https://www.dailymail.co.uk/health/article-5232351/Teen-girls-pressure-boys-send-nude-photos.html.

[15] Chris McCormack, 'Society: The pervasive and pernicious online porn epidemic', *News Weekly*, April 6, 2019, http://www.newsweekly.com.au/article.php?id=58479.

[16] Shane James O'Neill, 'Mental Health, Depression, Suicide, and Pornography', *Proven Men,* January 31, 2019, https://www.provenmen.org/mental-health-depression-suicide-pornography-2.

[17] 'How the Porn Industry Capitalizes on the Loneliness and Depression of its Consumers', *Fight the New Drug,* October 10, 2019, https://fightthenewdrug.org/why-porn-leaves-you-lonelier-than-before.

[18] Peg Steep, 'What Porn Can Do to Intimacy', *Psychology Today*, July 16, 2014, https://www.psychologytoday.com/au/blog/tech-support/201407/what-porn-does-intimacy.

[19] McCormack, 'Online porn epidemic'.

[20] Covenant Eyes, *Porn Stats: 250+ facts, quotes, and statistics about pornography use* (Owosso, MI: Covenant Eyes, 2018), https://www.covenanteyes.com/pornstats.

[21] Krocs On, 'Feminists march against Rape Culture', YouTube, July 18, 2018, https://youtu.be/AsLpR0XPfNst.

[22] 'The Candace Owens Show: Michael Knowles', July 14, 2019, https://www.prageru.com/video/the-candace-owens-show-michael-knowles.

[23] Nicola Davis, 'Less sex please, we're millennials – study', *The Guardian*, August 23, 2016, https://www.theguardian.com/lifeandstyle/2016/aug/02/less-sex-please-were-millennials-study.

[24] Owens, 'Michael Knowles'.

[25] 'Italian men suffer 'sexual anorexia' after Internet porn use', *ANSA.IT,* March 4, 2019, http://www.ansa.it/web/notizie/rubriche/english/2011/02/24/visualizza_new.html_1583160579.html.

[26] Owens, 'Michael Knowles'.

[27] Chastity Project, 'Sexuality'.

[28] An allusion to the classic *Peter Pan* by J. M. Barrie.

[29] Chastity Project, 'Sexuality'.

[30] 'America's Not-So-Secret Addiction', Slightly Offens*ve, YouTube, Dec 14, 2019, https://www.youtube.com/watch?v=2cO78JajYt4&t=1591s.

[31] Alex Hawkins, 'XHamster Report on Digital Sexuality, Part:1', XHamster, viewed July 27, 2019, https://xhamster.com/blog/posts/934387.
[32] Instagram, Mattxiv, Matt Bernstein, accessed July 24, 2019.

Training Soldiers for War

— 4 —

The aim of military training is not just to prepare men for battle, but to make them long for it.

– Louis Simpson

THE LAST CHAPTER WAS PRETTY HEAVY going. Now that we have established that we are under some serious and deadly assault, it should spur us on to take up arms and fight for our families, our sons and our daughters, and our homes (see Neh. 4:14). We must learn to use our spiritual weapons of warfare, not just to be on the defensive but to turn the tables and start pushing back the kingdom of darkness.

We are in a battle, whether we choose to be engaged or not. Christ Jesus, in obedience, was sent from the Father into enemy territory, behind enemy lines, and won the battle. He was victorious for mankind and for His Father. He then ascended into heaven and sent us His Holy Spirit, the same Spirit who guided and empowered Him. We as Christ followers are to advance God's kingdom on earth and push back the powers of darkness—and we have been given the power and authority to do so.

The question is, *Will we engage or not?*

This chapter explores discipleship. It's helpful to look at this through the perspective of training soldiers for war, as I believe there are some useful parallels for understanding the process and importance of discipleship training.

I begin with a personal account.

I remember well my first day of army basic training as a freckled-faced young country girl. We signed on the dotted line in the presence of warm and friendly army recruitment officers, waved farewell to our loved ones, and boarded the bus for the short thirty-minute drive to the training base, chatting all the way in excited anticipation. We reached the base, and the bus pulled to a steady stop. Before we knew what was happening, angry corporals boarded and started yelling and ordering us out of the bus as if we were convicts arriving at a prison camp.

In all naivety, I was expecting a warm welcome, a cup of tea, maybe some sort of appreciation for signing up to serve our country for the next three years. But the hostile reception was a blow. *What the heck have I just done?* We were tricked!

The relentless angry shouting of orders along with being forced to line up, commanded not to speak, and marched around together all day as we collected our issued items was a shock. Considering that we didn't know how to march, we looked absurd. We were out of step and messy, and I thought it was unnecessary and ridiculous. The instructors were so serious and intense that I found it quite amusing. I can remember at one point they suddenly ordered us to stop, and we all ran into the back of each other. It was funny, and in a moment of forgetfulness I laughed out loud. The instructor singled me out and tore me to shreds, making an example of me in front of the group. Unfortunately, I had to endure many such humiliations before I finally learned to control myself and remain steely no matter what the circumstance.

RESOCIALISATION

When a young person joins the army and signs on the dotted line, he doesn't automatically become a soldier. It takes a lot of mental and physical training. Perhaps the hardest part is the resocialisation process one goes through, from an attitude of putting *me first* to one of a loyal and responsible team member who continually puts the group needs ahead of his own and obeys orders instantly. The resocialisation process is 'the tearing down and rebuilding an individual's role and socially constructed sense of self'.[1] The old identity is stripped away, and the new identity comes forth. At the end of basic training, the emerging person has the disposition and the discipline of a soldier and is set on a path to further training and specialisation.

The first step of resocialisation is stripping away the outward identity of the recruit. This is done by cutting the hair, issuing a uniform, lining up, and going everywhere in group formation. There are no individuals. Everyone looks the same and does the same thing and is subordinate to the same people, who seem to be always angry and yelling. A common oppressor brings unity to the oppressed.

In the process of resocialisation at military basic training, the recruit gains new values, attitudes, and skills essential to every soldier. After graduating, he goes on to specialise in a combat role, such as infantry, artillery, armour, cavalry, or field engineers, or a noncombat support role, such as ordinance, medical, or intelligence. A soldier must learn drills and actions until they become second nature. He is continually learning and training because war could break out at any time and defence technology is constantly evolving into more high-tech capabilities—what was learned last year may be obsolete now.

A new sense of self-confidence is gained through completing military training. Self-confidence is an assurance of your abilities or values.[2] It increases self-esteem, or how you feel about yourself. Self-confidence doesn't come through ego or estimating you are smart, cool, or better than others in some way but through experience. It is earned. Michael Anthony, in his article '8 Navy SEAL Tips for More Self-Confidence', writes:

> Imagine a soldier. A soldier goes through training, he's put in uncomfortable positions, pushed beyond his limits, he doesn't cling to results, only growth. He repeats his training again and again, "The more we bleed in peace, the less we bleed in war." He continually pushes himself. He doesn't mask his fear or insecurity and he acts courageously in the face of that fear. He is self-confident not because of his ego, but because of his experiences. Through training and hard work he's come to believe in himself. He learns that "I can," and eventually "I can" becomes his routine. This is the true heart of self-confidence.[3]

So, what's the point of all this? The point is that when a person is converted to faith in Christ, like a brand-new army recruit, he needs to go through a resocialisation process to help him strip away the old habits, values, and attitudes that controlled the way he lived his life up until then and how he estimated himself. He learns a new code of conduct and learns to obey His Commander. He has a military manual called the Bible to help him, and he has been thoroughly orientated with how to constantly use it. He needs to be continually training and learning, building in the confidence of his identity and his capabilities, using the spiritual weapons of warfare—the ones that are mighty in pulling down strongholds (2 Cor. 10:4). The training involves mentors and others who are gifted for teaching and instructing to help new followers mature.

LOST BOYS

He needs to understand that we are in a state of spiritual war that will not cease in his lifetime.

> No soldier in active service gets entangled in the [ordinary business] affairs of civilian life; [he avoids them] so that he may please the one who enlisted him to serve. - 2 Tim. 2:4 (AMP)

The discipleship process is like military basic training. Many new Christians, mere babes in the faith, have not gone through a thorough resocialisation (discipleship) process and, therefore, are not able to walk victoriously in their new identity in Christ. They have not been adequately orientated with the Bible, nor do they understand the power of Scripture. They have had no spiritual weaponry training and lack the disposition and discipline of a disciple. Like immature babes, they can neither give an answer for their faith nor a good reason to hold on to their faith in this prevailing culture. To them, the church is irrelevant and stuck in the past. They lack Christian confidence and self-esteem. In this weak state they have been easy prey for the enemy to carry them off into captivity or else allow them to wander around aimlessly and ineffectually.

Discipleship is crucial. Just because someone is raised in a Christian home and educated in a Christian school doesn't mean they have been adequately trained to maturity. Many Christian parents are ill-trained themselves. The spirit of this age has very effective capabilities to resocialise our children.

Training Soldiers for War

Recently, I listened to someone teaching about discipleship. He explained that discipleship is about instruction. The process of instruction is to build structures first so that one can receive information or teaching. This means discipline must be learned to receive the teaching, and this starts in the home. Children cannot learn at school if they are ill-disciplined and out of control; their learning is inhibited.

Likewise, military basic training builds the structures inside of the new recruit through discipline, correction, punishment, and so on. When the structures have been built, learning can then take place, and the recruit graduates to professional soldier. If he fails to learn the basic discipline or skills, he repeats the training until he can meet the requirements.

Paul's letter to the Colossians says to 'admonish' and 'teach' one another, so that believers can become mature (Col. 3:16). *Admonish* means to rebuke, to warn, to instruct through warning and critique, not unlike the continual training of soldiers, particularly during recruit training. Both in the home and in the church, there is a need for more teaching and admonishing to build strong warriors.

LEARNING WARFARE

Training also involves studying warfare and understanding the nature of war.

LOST BOYS

The Australian Army description of war goes like this:

> The nature of conflict remains enduring; however, its characteristics have and will continue to change. AC-FLOC acknowledges the Clausewitzean view of war as being dynamic, unpredictable, difficult to control and therefore chaotic.[4]

The nature of war, or conflict, doesn't change, but the character of war is dynamic, constantly changing, and we must be continually adapting and contextualising strategies. Sometimes it will seem chaotic, particularly in situations where we have just discovered another battlefront that has opened up or where the adversary has been covertly making progress. However, we must prevail.

The enemy is extremely active with capabilities that are confusing our children, such as the porn strategy and the new gender theory. Like the Iraqi army in the Battle of Medina Ridge in Operation Desert Storm, our tanks and artillery seem to be facing the wrong direction as we are bombarded by the enemy. The culture of this generation is unique. More complexities exist than in pre-technology days without internet and smartphones, and the issues young people face are huge. Access to information has exploded. We are living through a technological revolution that doesn't seem to stop. The standard answers we give to young people who are under intense fire and ambushed at every turn are no longer adequate.

The military has a planning tool template, known by its acronym SMEAC, that every leader learns: Situation,

Mission, Execution, Administration, Command, and Communications. It is an extremely effective tool for delivering clear and precise orders for a mission—so effective in fact, that it is now being adopted in the corporate business world, as you will see by doing a quick internet search.

To plan a mission, a military leader must first look at the *situation*. This involves intelligence gathering to ascertain the location and movement of the enemy forces, the weaponry and capability available to the enemy, and the strength of the force. It also involves information on friendly forces, such as who they are, where they are located, their movements, their capabilities, and so on. The friendlies include adjacent units or battalions, supporting units, or higher formations. In addition, there is also intelligence gathering that contributes to the planning of a mission.

Imagine going into a battle not only untrained (or not adequately discipled) but uninformed and blind to what the enemy is doing or his movements and capabilities. Envision entering a battle with allies (other churches or Christian organisations and groups) but no communication or deliberate cooperation or collaboration. Could World War I or II have been won with every Allied force doing its own thing?

Definitely not.

LOST BOYS

Training warriors for warfare is vital. Intelligence gathering is crucial, and collaborating with allies or battalions is paramount.

---

[1] Ashley Crossman, 'Understanding Resocialization in Sociology', ThoughtCo., August 28, 2019. https://www.thoughtco.com/resocialization-3026522.
[2] Collins Dictionary, s.v. 'self-confidence', accessed October 8, 2019, https://www.collinsdictionary.com/dictionary/english/self-confidence.
[3] Michael Anthony, '8 Navy SEAL Tips for More Self-Confidence', The Good Men Project, January 15, 2014, https://goodmenproject.com/featured-content/mru-8-navy-seal-tips-for-more-self-confidence.
[4] Head Modernisation and Strategic Planning – Army Australian Army Headquarters, *Army's Future Land Operating Concept*, September 2009, https://www.army.gov.au/sites/default/files/acfloc_2012_main.pdf, 4.

Weapon Training

— 5 —

I am not afraid of an army of lions led by a sheep; I am afraid of an army of sheep led by a lion.

– Alexander the Great

AFTER A FEW YEARS IN THE ARMY, I was sent on a promotion course. It felt like basic training again. We were marched around everywhere, confined to the barracks, and subject to random room inspections, rigorous physical training, bush training, weapon handling, and lots of drills. And of course, the yelling and the screaming of orders was constant.

The army had recently passed a new policy that women were to march with weapons, so we had to learn weapon drill for the first time. Not only did we now carry a rifle for drill, the old heavy SLRs, but we were also issued with a bayonet that fixed onto the end of the rifles.

We were told exactly where to put everything in our locker, and the bayonet given to us in a metal scabbard was to be placed in a certain position on top of the locker. And there it stayed for weeks, as we'd not been instructed to use it or do anything with it at that stage. Since this was the first time we'd ever touched a bayonet, we didn't even pull it out of its scabbard.

About three weeks into the course, very early one morning the instructors appeared at our barracks for a random room inspection. This wasn't unusual; we were used to the mad panic to get things straightened up (or hidden) quickly and stand by our beds silently. We were two to a room in alphabetical order. I was McGarvie, and my roommate was Musomechi. No personalised names were used. As we listened to the inspection going on a few rooms down, we heard a lot of angry yelling and the sound of metal drawn out of a scabbard. We looked at each other in horror—they were inspecting bayonets! We both had not even drawn our bayonet from its scabbard since we got it. Nobody had. Even if we had, we would not have known how to clean or polish it or keep it in good order. And besides, how many girls have an interest in big knives like bayonets?

I was sweating in terror. *Please, please, please, God, let my bayonet be okay!*

Weapon Training

Three inspectors walked into our room, one taking notes. The sergeant looked at us, one to the other, with distain. 'So who do we have here? McGarvie and Musomechi.'

He glared at Musomechi as he walked to her locker and grabbed her bayonet on top without even taking his eyes from her. She was almost sweating blood as she stared straight ahead at attention. He ripped the bayonet out of the scabbard. What?! The blade was clean, oiled, and sparkling! Musomechi was as shocked as he was. The sergeant didn't miss a beat, 'Good work, Musomechi,' he blurted. Then he turned to me.

Please, please, God, help me!

He reached up, grabbed the bayonet, then pulled the handle. The bayonet flew out of the scabbard in a puff of red dust. It was literally covered with rust! It looked like some relic dug up from the Great War. I almost fainted, but since I was a trained soldier, I had no expression on my face. Only the briefest bulging of my eyes and the slightest stiffening of my frame would have given away any reaction to the expert eye.

The sergeant threw the bayonet down on the floor in front of me in disgust. He then sprayed me with colourful insults, interjected with expletives, about how I was a disgrace to the army, my platoon, my corp, and myself and how I'd let everyone down, how I wasn't fit for military service, and on and on. He then assigned me my punishment of extra duties and walked out to claim his next victim.

I was mortified. It wasn't fair. But who said life was fair?

The rusty bayonet left a permanent stain where it hit the floor and was a daily reminder to me of the horror of not cleaning my weapon.

Weapon training and maintenance is the basic 101 for every soldier. The recruit who joins the army, whether for a combat role or not, needs to learn how to use and maintain the basic assault rifle.

For soldiers who specialise in combat roles, their rifle is everything. It is described as 'the only weapon which stands between them and death'. Marine Brigadier General H. Rupertus said those words in 1942 after the bombing of Pearl Harbor. Then he wrote the famous Rifleman's Creed, which he felt needed to be 'something so deep, a conviction so great, a faith so lasting that no one should have to be preached to about it' so that it would become basic instinct to any frontline soldier.[1]

This is the 'Rifleman's Creed' that every marine must learn by heart:

> This is my rifle. ... My rifle is my best friend. It is my life. I must master it as I must master my life. ... Without my rifle, I am useless. I must fire my rifle true. I must shoot straighter than my enemy who is trying to kill me. I must shoot him before he shoots me. ... My rifle and myself know that what counts in

Weapon Training

this war is not the rounds we fire, the noise of our burst, nor the smoke we make. We know that it is the hits that count. ... My rifle is ... my life. Thus, I will learn it as a brother. I will learn its weaknesses, its strength, its parts, its accessories, its sights and its barrel. I will ever guard it against the ravages of weather and damage as I will ever guard my legs, my arms, my eyes and my heart against damage. I will keep my rifle clean and ready. We will become part of each other. ... Before God, I swear this creed. My rifle and myself are the defenders of my country. We are the masters of our enemy. We are the saviors of my life. ... So be it, until victory ... and there is no enemy, but peace![2]

Soldiers have their weapons checked continually to ensure they are clean and in good working order, or else the success of battles and lives are at stake. Taking care of your rifle must become basic instinct. This is so important that soldiers can receive major punishment if their weapon is found to be with one speck of rust, carbon, or dirt.

Even as a young army nurse I learned to strip and assemble a rifle extremely fast. I knew every part and how to correct basic malfunctions and clean it. I was one of the fastest in my training group at loading magazines, and I discovered that I had a natural eye for firing on target.

But professional soldiers who are true warriors are machines. They are incredibly skilled and adept at using their rifles and many other weapons of warfare. They have been trained so well and practice continually that whatever they do seems effortless and without a second thought. They are confident and steady, do not panic or run in fear, and are brave and courageous. These soldiers look out for each other, with no man left behind. Their fine motor skills are trained so well that, under the terrorising fear of battle, their muscle memory kicks in automatically even if they are in shock or fright. They have been trained *to fight rather than flee* when confronted with the real-life terror of battle and horrors that surround them.[3] Everyone is a valuable member of the team. They are family, and the mission comes first above personal needs or wants. The self-discipline and the group discipline are outstanding.

There's a lot to be learned from the discipline of a soldier who has been trained well and is in constant training. Imagine if Christians were trained like this. Read the 'Rifleman's Creed' again, and replace the words 'my rifle' with 'God's Truth' and 'God's Weapons'. It's a little clunky in places but powerful nonetheless.

Without God's Truth I am useless.

The Spartans were known for the skill and discipline of their soldiers. In war they would adopt a tight rectangular formation named the *Greek phalanx* that provided secure protection with interlocking shields. Each man also had a spear along with his breastplate, helmet, and greaves, or leg armour.[4] At the front were the battle-experienced strong warriors, in the middle were the

Weapon Training

inexperienced youth, and in the back rows were the experienced but aged soldiers up to sixty years. This formation provided safety and protection in the battle and prevented the young inexperienced warriors from fleeing in terror. Fleeing made the individual an easy target for the enemy, with no protection for their back, and breaking rank could lose the entire battle. The soldiers at the front demonstrated fighting skill and courage to the young soldiers. The older soldiers at the back kept the morale and encouraged the younger ones to stand firm.

I once heard a story about the Northern Ireland conflict when the IRA obtained rocket-propelled grenades (RPGs) from Russia. Since they didn't know how to operate these weapons—because they couldn't read the instructions written in Russian—the rockets failed to explode when they hit their targets. It wasn't until a British officer made a joke of it publicly and unwittingly disclosed the correct process for firing that the IRA learned what to do.[5]

In a game of paintball skirmish with my warmongering family, I found myself trapped behind a log under heavy fire when my weapon malfunctioned. Since I didn't really listen to the weapon-handling instructions before the game, I couldn't work out how to identify the problem to fix it. Fortunately, one of the staff who was playing on our side came to my rescue by making a heroic dash, skidding in beside me. Expert as he was, he quickly identified the most common problem; I had my safety catch engaged. Most embarrassing.

Imagine a battalion carrying a deadly weapon they couldn't use because they didn't know how to use it, or soldiers wandering around disorganised and undisciplined in a battle zone, oblivious to reality, or with weapons malfunctioning because they didn't know how to clean or maintain them. The weapons would be only useful for a few skirmishes before malfunctioning. What commander of a nation would send soldiers to war without providing them with effective weapons to fight, and more superior ones at that?

I fear that this is the situation of many Christians today. We don't know who we are, we have no idea that we are currently at war, and we don't know how to use our weapons of warfare or even what they look like. Many of us have our safety switch permanently engaged. Discipleship is key to training spiritual warriors to stand firm with confidence and take back ground.

> *For the weapons of our battle are not of flesh but are enormously powerful, capable of destroying fortresses.*
>
> *– 2 Cor. 10:4 NAB*

[1] 'My Rifle: The Creed of a US Marine', MarineParents.com, accessed June 20, 2019, https://www.marineparents.com/marinecorps/mc-rifle.asp.
[2] 'My Rifle'.
[3] Melissa Healy, 'In Face of Death—What Makes Soldiers Disregard Instinct?: Training: Reflex, loyalty and hatred of the enemy can be cultivated to ensure that GIs fight instead of flee', *Los Angeles Times*, February 26, 1991, https://www.latimes.com/archives/la-xpm-1991-02-26-mn-2120-story.html.
[4] Joshua J. Mark, 'The Greek Phalanx', *Ancient History Encyclopedia*, January 18, 2012, https://www.ancient.eu/article/110/the-greek-phalanx.
[5] The source of this story cannot be found, but the IRA was suspected to have 40 RPG-7s in a 1996 estimate of their inventory.
https://www.pbs.org/wgbh/pages/frontline/shows/ira/inside/weapons.html.

Feminisation Stifles Masculinity

— 6 —

In today's church, the gospel is no longer about saving the world against impossible odds. It's about finding a happy relationship with a wonderful man.

– David Murrow, author of *Why Men Hate Going to Church*

WHERE DOES ONE START ON THIS TOPIC? Perhaps an overview of the situation as to the state of our men and boys in the church.

The situation is that men, in a sweeping generalisation, dislike going to church.

In Australia, 60 percent of church attendees are female. In every age group and every denomination, women outnumber men.[1] I would hazard a guess that 20 percent of those male church goers are attending just to please their wives.

> 93 percent of senior pastors in America are men, according to evangelical pollster George Barna. But, the majority of attendees in a typical church are women. Barna goes so far as to refer to women as 'the backbone of the Christian congregations in America.'[2]

To put these findings in perspective, think about this: 'On any given Sunday there are 13 million more adult women than men in America's churches'.[3]

Thirteen million more women.

A recent article from ABC News titled, 'Australia's "man drought" is real-especially if you're a Christian woman looking for love', highlights this phenomenon. The article describes the demographics of the 'man drought', explaining that even though there are 98.6 men to every 100 women, this gap widens if you are a Christian woman searching for a husband with the same values, because 'women are more likely than men to report being Christian'.[4]

Off the top of my head, I could name a significant number of men, both young and old, who are totally disengaged and find church attendance a painful experience. And I keep running into Christian friends from years ago who have joined that ever-growing diaspora of churchless Christians.

Feminisation Stifles Masculinity

Researchers believe many factors contribute to the male/female imbalance of church attendance, one of the main ones being that the church no longer relates to men's sense of duty, sacrifice, challenge, risk-taking, fighting for a noble cause, chivalry, and so on. What men seek and respect most is 'a mighty, conquering king to suffer, rather than cuddle, with'.[5] The feminine imagery of a romantic, intimate relationship, a husband to protect, *just Jesus and me* attitude is individualistic, appeals more to women, and is very inward looking.

Brett and Kate McKay, in their thought-prevoking article titled 'The Feminization of Christianity',[6] discuss how the individual *just Jesus and me* attitude sends the message that faith is a personal spirituality only and does not intersect with the wider world in domains such as business, politics, the arts, education, or even building flourishing cities. They also discuss the lack of virility and masculine role models in the church.

Young boys love heroes. Look at the superhero popularity with boys; they long for masculine champions fighting for good and saving the world. Boys are preparing for the adventure of their lives and need to learn to forge forth and conquer.

We raised our boys on the mission field of Africa. My husband built them a sandpit of sorts. Our friends back in Australia would send us endless packs of those little green army men, which our sons loved. The packs contained infantry men, tanks, and artillery. The boys would spend hours and hours every day, after school or on weekends, setting up elaborate battlefields and fighting each other. I was truly amazed how they never seemed to tire of it. As they got older, they graduated to handmade wooden swords. I remember watching an old home video of the boys and their mates sword fighting. It just went on and on at every available location—around the yard, in the house, outside the yard, on the roof, in the garage. They played with their friends, on their own, on the road, at the neighbors, ad nauseam. And this was one of their favourite pastimes. Then came the pellet guns and the air rifles. Then the motorbikes …

Boys were born for adventure and to change the world. We are called to forge forth, to conquer to build cities and to advance God's kingdom on earth.

Once boys become young men in the church, the options they see to follow our mighty, conquering King are narrowed to youth pastor or worship leader (both revered in the church as high callings); play or sing on the worship team; Sunday school teacher; youth leader; small group leader; and so on. What about changing culture? Fighting a cause? Starting a business? Building a city? Helping the oppressed? Serving our country in military or government? Influencing a workplace to make it flourish? Creating a masterpiece? Writing a book? Inventing something or designing better ways to lift society?

Feminisation Stifles Masculinity

In the McKay article, the authors argue that in modern sermons

> there is less emphasis on the need to suffer, struggle, and sacrifice for the gospel and for others, and more emphasis on how the gospel can be a tool towards greater self-realization and personal fulfilment. The gospel is not presented as heroic challenge, but therapy. ... One 19th century YMCA speaker declared that the Christian gospel had become 'too easy and too cheap', where what men really longed for was the promise of 'battles instead of feasts, swords instead of prizes, campaigns instead of comforts'.[7]

In the book of 2 Samuel 11, we read the story of David and Bathsheba. David was lounging around at home when he 'arose from his bed' to go for a walk on the roof of his palace, and behold, there was Bathsheba. David wasn't supposed to be idle; we are told that it happened in spring during the time when kings (along with their men) were supposed to go out to war. David's men were out doing the hard yards of besieging a city. This was tedious work and could take months or longer. Think digging in, blocking supplies, keeping watch 24-7, preventing troops escaping, waiting it out so that the inhabitants become totally demoralised through starvation, thirst, or disease. David may have been skipping the boring part and going out to the battle for the final push, the exciting part at the due time. After all, he'd already killed his tens of thousands.

LOST BOYS

When men aren't going out to war to fight a noble cause, they become vulnerable in their idleness. Easy targets.

Thy kingdom come is about together advancing God's kingdom of righteousness on earth. The term 'kingdom of God' is often replaced with 'family of God' in a more feminine expression,[8] the former being more mission oriented, and the latter more relational. Yet we are a part of God's plan to advance His kingdom on earth. We are on a mission.

Christian music, too, has been criticised as becoming more feminised. Contemporary praise and worship has been often bemoaned as 'vague and dreamy sentimentality'.[9] Although appealing to some men, many contemporary songs are a turn-off for others. Worship has changed from the old hymns *about* God to the present-day praise and worship songs sung *to* God.

A *Biola Magazine* article states that as a result of the feminisation of Christian worship, 'many people think of the church only as a nurturing place that addresses personal needs. ... Think: sitting in circles, sharing feelings, holding hands, singing softly, comforting members'.[10]

It is also important to note in this discussion that research has found that 'when a mother comes to Christ, her family will join her at church only 17 percent of the time; but when a father comes to Christ, his family joins him 93 percent of the time'.[11]

It appears that our adversary knows this.

Feminisation Stifles Masculinity

As I thought about these astounding figures, I reflected on my own upbringing. I was one of six children raised in a very traditional church family. My father, a cattleman, horseman, and hardworking man of the land, was the spiritual leader of our home and very devout. My mother initially had a nominal faith, less devout than my father—however, she is now a woman of deep faith whom I greatly admire. During my childhood, every morning when I awoke, I could hear my father in the living room on his knees praying his prayers. Every night we had to kneel and pray prayers as a family before going to bed. I didn't like it one bit. And yet today, in our middle age, you will find every one of his children in church each Sunday. I have a new appreciation for my father, as he has led his wife and children to walk in his ways.

OUTSIDE THE CHURCH

And finally, a word about the feminisation of our boys in Western society outside the church.

Through the education and media establishments, our kids are now being taught gender theory, which purports that gender is socially constructed. Masculinity is being extinguished before our eyes. Sex and gender are being separated, and primary-aged children are being taught that despite being born with male or female genitalia, it does not define one's gender.[12]

LOST BOYS

An article by Spencer Klavan titled 'Be a Man' talks about how a military dictator in ancient times subdued a people group. Klavan begins by stating that 'gender theorists know what they are doing when they target children. We should know what we are doing when we fight back'. Think about this:

> In the late 500s BC, the military dictator Aristodemus took over the Greek colony of Cumae. He slaughtered his enemies en masse and undertook to ensure that no Cumaean man would ever be more than his slave. Here is how he did it, according to the essayist Dionysius of Halicarnassus. 'To ensure that no noble or manly aspiration would arise in any of the citizens, he decided to feminize every young man by means of his upbringing in the city's schools.' Aristodemus had the boys of Cumae wear long hair and embroidered gowns; he made them listen to soft music and keep out of the sun; he starved them of adult male guidance. This was so none of them would ever grow up strong enough to stand against him.[13]

It is time to stand against this assault on masculinity to ensure that indeed 'noble [and] manly aspirations would arise' and flourish. Society needs this more than ever.

As an aside, I was intrigued by the mention of the role of *city schools* in the tactics of the dictator Aristodemus to subdue and disempower boys, because strong male guidance in our city schools is apparently lacking. Women in the education sector outnumber men considerably. In Australia, women make up 97 percent of early learning

Feminisation Stifles Masculinity

staff, 82 percent of primary teachers and 60 percent of secondary teachers.[14] This means that many children will likely have little to no adult male guidance in their entire schooling years. With the growing fatherlessness epidemic and the lack of male role models in schools, these figures are of deepest concern for our boys.

Added to this, as part of the normal socialisation process, girls learn *emotional intelligence*, while boys learn *heroic intelligence.*[15] This heroic intelligence is how boys grow to be respected as men who protect and lead their families. It appears that heroic intelligence in this age of gender confusion and the extinguishing of true masculinity has successfully neutered scores of our strong young men. And the education system is complicit.

Many of us have watched the film *Hacksaw Ridge,* the story of how a young medic by the name of Desmond Doss won a Medal of Honor in the Second World War. Because of his religious beliefs as a Seventh Day Adventist, he refused to carry a weapon or to work on the Sabbath. The film portrays him as a somewhat good-looking young man; however, in real life, as we observe in his interviews for documentaries, he was an awkward scrawny guy with a slow southern drawl that made him appear intellectually challenged. He didn't carry the typical hero persona. Yet this skinny, physically weak guy who never compromised his faith and values became a hero. When troops withdrew from a failed assault on

LOST BOYS

Hacksaw Ridge under intense fire from the Japanese, Doss refused to leave the wounded and stayed. In a twelve-hour period he single-handedly rescued seventy-five wounded and dying men. With bullets flying around him and covered from head to foot in blood, he crawled on his belly in the dirt searching for the wounded. He would then drag his comrades to the edge of the escarpment, tie a rope around their chest and shoulders, and lower them to the ground to safety. Over the twelve-hour period that he stayed up there, he averaged one rescue every ten minutes. Doss said that he prayed the whole time, 'Lord please, help me get one more!'[16]

What selfless heroism and chivalry! May this be the prayer of all Christians for our lost boys, *Lord, just one more!*

I end this chapter with a story that highlights the incredible, heroic risk-taking that men do for the sake of protecting women and children, another situation where manly aspirations arose and won the day.

On June 23rd, 2018, a Thai soccer team of boys and their twenty-five-year-old coach were trapped about four kilometres inside a cave by flooding rains. This happened at the early start of the monsoon season. The boys and their coach, thirteen in all, were found by two incredibly brave British divers a week later stranded on a narrow rock shelf inside the cave. The challenge was how to extricate the group from the cave with obstacles of rising water and decreasing oxygen levels. Governments from USA, China, Britain, Australia, and other parts of the world sent in expert teams to assist in the rescue. Thousands of people, mostly men, were involved. They worked together to plan a way to rescue the boys, considering options such as keeping the boys alive until the monsoon season ended, which would be months away, to drilling a shaft into the cave to rescue them. They tried pumping water out of the cave, but with the continual rains and other problems, this was not going to be the solution. A Thai Navy Seal trained diver lost his life while delivering air cylinders to the boys, a devastating blow to morale.

It was two Australian men, experienced cave divers, Richard Harris, an anesthetist, and retired veterinarian Craig Challen, who 'masterminded one of the most remarkable rescues the world has ever seen'.[17] The entire group of boys were rescued safely with huge risk to both the boys and the rescuers. The boys were put to sleep so they wouldn't panic underwater, and their hands were bound so they wouldn't try to rip off their masks. They were then carried and handled through the cave system, much of it submersed under water with nil visibility, all four kilometres, by a team of divers and rescuers. It was indeed a daring rescue.

These men had to consider the risks, the possibility of losing one or more of the children. What if it didn't work? How many boys were they willing to lose before they would give up? If they lost any, would they be held accountable by the Thai government for manslaughter? The Australian government was still in the process of securing an agreement with the Thai government when oxygen levels in the cave dropped dangerously low and they had to go ahead without that needed assurance. What if they lost their own lives or the lives of others during the rescue attempt?

Richard Harris and Craig Challen were both awarded 2019 Australian of the Year. They are not macho men, but they typify the characteristics of masculinity so well: risk takers, brave, confident, and resourceful. They described this harrowing experience as 'an adventure of a lifetime'.[18]

Bring on more noble and manly aspirations of heroism like this. The world needs it. The church needs it. Boys need it.

The previous two chapters highlighted the need to disciple our young men into strong warriors to strengthen them against attack from *the flesh, the world, and the devil.*

This chapter is a warning that we must stop feminising our boys so they can grow up to their full masculine potential. Primarily it highlights the need for the church to defeminise their expression of faith equipping and releasing young men to the adventure of their lifetime following the conquering King out to war.

Make Christianity masculine again.

---

[1] Ruth Powell, 'Fact: More Women go to church than men', *Eternity*, August 2, 2017, https://www.eternitynews.com.au/australia/fact-more-women-go-to-church-than-men.
[2] Holly Pivec, 'The Feminization of the Church: Why Its Music, Message and Ministries Are Driving Men Away', *Biola Magazine*, Spring 2006, http://magazine.biola.edu/article/06-spring/the-feminization-of-the-church.
[3] 'Why Men Matter - Both now and forever: A Look at the Numbers About Men and Men's Ministry', Washington Area Coalition of Men's Ministries (WACMM), accessed October 20, 2019, http://www.wacmm.org/Stats.html.
[4] Karen Tong, 'Australia's "man drought" is real – especially if you're a Christian woman looking for love', *ABC News*, November 8, 2019, https://www.abc.net.au/news/2019-11-08/australia-talks-man-drought-real-especially-for-christian-women/11682002.
[5] Brett & Kate McKay, 'The Feminization of Christianity', The Art of Manliness, accessed November 8, 2019, https://www.artofmanliness.com/articles/the-feminization-of-christianity.
[6] McKay, 'Feminization of Christianity.'
[7] McKay, 'Feminization of Christianity.'
[8] McKay, 'Feminization of Christianity.'
[9] McKay, 'Feminization of Christianity.'
[10] Pivec, 'The Feminization of the Church.'
[11] 'Why Men Matter', WACMM.
[12] 'Genderbread Person v4.0: A teaching tool for the big concept of breaking gender down into bite-sized, digestible pieces', The Genderbread Person, accessed November 18, 2019. https://www.genderbread.org.
[13] Spencer Klavan, 'Be a Man', The American Mind, November 6, 2019, https://americanmind.org/post/be-a-man.
[14] Jack Graham, 'Men don't feel welcome in early childhood. Here's how to change that', *apolitical*, May 8, 2018, https://apolitical.co/solution_article/men-not-welcome-gender-inequality-in-the-early-childhood-profession.
[15] *The Boy Crisis*, 31
[16] *Hacksaw Ridge: The True Basic Movie of the Sabbath Keeper,* Desmond Doss, June 24, 2018, https://www.youtube.com/watch?v=WrchEkT_CUA.
[17] David Penberthy, 'Dirty little secret: cave rescue became an adventure of a lifetime', *The Australian*, Nov 15, 2019, 3.
[18] Penberthy, 'Dirty little secret.'

Engaging the Intellect

— 7 —

I do not feel obliged to believe that the same God who has endowed us with senses, reason and intellect has intended us to forego their use.

– Galileo Galilei

IN 2018 AT THE O2 ARENA IN LONDON, up to eight thousand people gathered for a public debate. Most of the audience were reportedly young males.[1] The *Guinness Book of World Records* is investigating this as the largest public debate in recent history.[2] In addition, it has received over four hundred thousand views on YouTube at the time of this writing. The media covered the debate, not so much for the content but for why so many young men would be drawn to such an event when usually the venue only receives those numbers of crowds for rock stars.

So, what was the topic?

It was about God and the legitimacy of holding on to religion in any form in our society today. Is religion and its ideas worth retiring as old and outdated, or are these ideas beneficial for the flourishing of mankind?

The debate involved Sam Harris, a high-profile neuroscientist, author, atheist, and philosopher, who argued that religious ideas are not needed for mankind's flourishing. Jordan Peterson, a psychology professor and author, argued that they were indeed needed. It was not so much a debate as a respectful and amicable discussion. If you haven't watched it, then it is worth your while to do so.

And why would so many people watch a two-hour intellectual debate online? A good movie, yes, but something that demands full concentration as you try to keep up with the cerebral discussion of two incredibly smart men? Why would young men be drawn to this?

In 2017, a four-part biblical series was released on YouTube. Each part was over two and a half hours long. This is perhaps the most-watched Bible series on YouTube ever. Part I has had 4.2 million views, Part II and III over 1 million views each, and Part IV has had 3.1 million views. Altogether that's 9.9 million views. This Bible series wasn't released by a theologian but by clinical psychologist Jordan Peterson.

Who around the world would a public debate on religion and a Bible series attract? It seems to be young men, and the mainstream media have been trying to work this out.

Engaging the Intellect

The title of a BBC article pretty much sums up this phenomenon: 'Why do young men worship Professor Jordan Peterson?'[3] Or the *Sydney Morning Herald*: 'Young men search for answers, rising star Jordan Peterson gives them'.[4] Or this: 'Why does Jordan Peterson appeal to so many young men?'[5]

By the way, Jordan Peterson doesn't call himself a Christian, as he thinks that's a relative term which can be interpreted in many ways. He prefers to say that he acts as if he believes God is real.

Jordan Peterson published an international best-selling book in 2018 titled *12 Rules of Life: An Antidote to Chaos*. This book has been 'devoured in particular by young men'.[6] What's it about? It's a book that encourages accountability and individual responsibility, a self-help book of sorts. The 12 Rules are very practical and commonsensical. 'Stand up straight with your shoulders back', 'always tell the truth', 'make your bed and clean your room', 'compare yourself to who you were yesterday, not who someone else is today', 'make friends with people who want the best for you', 'set your house in perfect order before you criticise anyone', and 'assume that the person you are listening to might know something you don't' are just some of them.[7]

Jordan Peterson speaks around the world in large auditoriums and stadiums, and tickets are sold out quickly. I've watched videos and heard accounts about how young men from the audience approach Peterson afterward, thanking him for helping them get their lives straightened out, marry the girl they were living with, start talking to their father after years of relationship breakdown, stop bad habits, and get a job, and even preventing them from suicide. Aren't these the types of things a young man might gain from a father figure? Or a pastor/minister/priest?

As stated, there has been much discussion in the media around the world about why young men are drawn to Peterson, and I think the primary reason is the need for the wise advice of a father figure to speak frankly and nonjudgmentally to young men. With this, I believe, are a couple of characteristics of high importance. First, he engages the mind and intellect, which seem to be lacking in educational institutions and the church. Second, Peterson gives real answers for navigating life while not glossing over the fact that the journey is inevitably filled with suffering and unfairness. He encourages young people to forge forth despite all this.

Let me explain each of these further.

Engaging the Mind and Intellect

I believe young men need and long to be engaged intellectually, and a vacuum exists in both the education system and many churches. Much can be said about the lack of intellectual rigor in the education system, and I touch on that in later chapters; however, for this discussion, I'll focus on the church. The church was once the place where the most brilliant scholars were raised, Great universities such as Harvard and Yale and many more were originally established as Christian learning institutions. Something has been lost, as young men are falling away by the score. Many of them accuse the church of being too emotional and superficial and lacking in intellectual rigor, particularly regarding apologetics, not providing robust biblical reasoning for the values and principles men have been taught to live by.

Nancy Pearcy, in her book *Total Truth: Liberating Christianity from Its Cultural Captivity*, provides an excellent discussion on the history of evangelicalism and its theological weaknesses and the lack of the cognitive side of religious practice. She describes that when evangelical groups broke away from the existing denominations, they 'tended to downplay the role of theology in favour of practical application such as personal devotion, moral living and social reform'.[8] Obviously all this is good and praiseworthy, however, there has been a *missing cognitive element* being felt today by many, including young people. The lack of strong theological teaching and engagement of the intellect in discipling young people has resulted in many Christians not being able to stand against the onslaught of secular, nihilistic arguments at universities or in the media.

LOST BOYS

Jeremy Boreing of *The Daily Wire* gave a great commentary on this situation:

> When you teach your children only caricatures of the arguments against your own position, you send them into battle worse than unarmed. You send them into battle against mechanized armies with wooden swords painted silver. And they think they are actually armed, and then they get out in the world and they hear actual smart arguments against what they believe, and they crumble. And when they crumble, they believe 'what my parents taught me is a lie because they led me like a sheep unto the slaughter'.[9]

When God moves in our soul, it activates a hunger, a desire to learn more, particularly spiritual and theological knowledge, and understanding how that translates into culture and how to live out our lives. We long for a foundational and solid reason for our faith and how we live it.

The revivalists of the colonial era focused on an intense conversion experience and in doing so relegated religion to be defined to the emotional realm.[10] This contributed to the neglect of doctrine as well as the whole works of hundreds of years of condensing biblical teaching as expressed corporately through statements of faith, creeds, and confessions by the best of the best theologians and scholars in history.

In addition to this, Pearcy goes on to say that with conversion becoming an emotional experience, religion was disconnected from the rational.[11] It is understandable how the emotional emphasis during the colonial era was a reaction to the spiritual coldness and indifference particularly in the religious culture of the day. Perhaps the reaction against the traditional ways was too huge a pendulum swing, where the baby was thrown out with the bath water.

Fast forward to the present, and we can see how emotionalism plays a significant role in evangelical churches. Church leaders have needed to be gifted or dramatic preachers, performers, and storytellers to stir hearts and evoke emotion to bring people to make life-changing decisions such as a 'conversion experience'. Today we see many evangelists, speakers, and Christian musicians with celebrity-like status. Yet, of late we have seen some very prominent Christian men who have publicly walked away from their faith. When the emotion and passion wear away in the highs and lows of life, together with the pull of the pleasures of the world, there is no rational anchor to keep one grounded in the Christian faith of truth and beauty.

The bottom line is that the church of today is not adequately engaging the minds of our youth, particularly young men.

REAL ANSWERS FOR NAVIGATING LIFE

Now to my second characteristic of the Peterson phenomena: Peterson provides genuine answers for navigating life, to forge forth, while not glossing over the fact that our lives are inevitably filled with suffering and unfairness. He has assumed a father-figure role to help young men confront the unknown chaos ahead of them and to deal with it.

Young reporter Luke Kinsella, in his article from news.com.au, wrote that he went online and watched several of Peterson's lectures and figured out why he believes young men are drawn to him, and I agree. He states:

> Dr. Peterson's message is a hard one to hear: "Life is suffering." Hardship is inevitable and life will always find some way to make you resentful. But don't complain about it, because that'll make it worse. Instead, find some reason to make life worth it, despite that suffering. ... Something terrible happens to you. Should you be angry? Bitter? Resentful? Well, you could be. And you'd probably have every right to be. But is that the answer? Maybe the answer is to find enough meaning in your life to bear your suffering, to carry it with you. Find a reason to keep going. Responsibility, he claims, is that reason. Being responsible for something or someone is what gives life meaning.[12]

Ben Shapiro gives his take on the reason for Peterson's popularity with young men, which is not dissimilar:

> Jordan Peterson says life is a struggle, life is chaotic, life is difficult. Go and forge forth in spite of those things, and this is what makes you a man, this is what makes you a woman. This is what makes you a person worthy of having freedom. This is

fundamentally a religious message in nature and an inspirational one.[13]

Boys in our Western societies have not been called out properly to *forge forth* with purpose. Nihilism, the belief that life is inherently meaningless, has become the new religion. It has replaced the Christian religious foundation of our Western civilisation. Nihilism, today's secular religion, does not provide boys with meaning, nor has it prepared them to be men. Young men are suffering from Peter Pan syndrome and are crippled and cannot progress from adolescence.[14]

The impetus of many young men to forge forth has been hindered by the spiritual, intellectual, physical, social, and emotional onslaught on every front. Young men need to be called to adventure and heroism. Due to the good times we currently enjoy in our wealthy societies, there is no necessity that would draw out this heroism. Depravation and challenge are what young people need to develop their character. Peterson encourages young men to courageously confront the unknown and speak the truth, and on life's adventure 'face the dragon', find the gold that it hides, and distribute it to the community.[15]

Peterson taps into that psychological need that young men have for courage, nobility and responsibility, because boys really do want to grow up to be heroic men. And they are hungry to have those discussions to understand what it looks like and how to get there.

LOST BOYS

Speaking about how young men are called out to forge forth in the adventure of life, he writes:

> Abraham was called out to an adventure. Young men die without that call to adventure. That's what attracts young people to ISIS. Their cause is warped because their ideology doesn't give them a moral equivalent to war. It hasn't called them out properly. Abraham was called out and experienced tyranny, famine, and conspiracies to steal his wife. God is calling us out to the great adventure of our life. It's not all happiness and roses and easy going. There is suffering, a noble cause, like an expedition. A call to a physical and spiritual adventure, to see if your values stack up against reality, like Abraham offering up Isaac.[16]

He also admonishes:

> Go somewhere you don't understand, go into the unknown ... Get away from your kindred, grow up! Get away from your family enough so that you can establish your independence. I've talked to people whose families have provided them with too much protection and they know it themselves, and that means they've been deprived of necessity. ... The Abrahamic story is a call to adventure. ... What moves you out of your father's house and the comforts of your home is a purpose beyond you.[17]

The call for adventure is in the heart of every young person, particularly boys. They need to understand that there is a transcendental purpose beyond themselves. Young men want to engage their intellect, they want to frankly discuss ideas and listen to those who have gone before. So that they go forth to life's battles fully armed and not with *wooden swords painted silver.*

---

[1] Mattha Busby, 'Harrison, Peterson and Murray: Inside the "Woodstock of debate"', *GQ*, July 17, 2018, https://www.gq-magazine.co.uk/article/sam-harris-jordan-peterson-douglas-murray-o2-2018.
[2] Douglas Murray, 'Arena talks in Dublin and London with Jordan Peterson, Sam Harris and Douglas Murray', *Spectator USA*, September 16, 2018, https://spectator.us/jordan-peterson-sam-harris-douglas-murray.
[3] Ben Bryant, 'Why do young men worship Professor Jordan Peterson?', *BBC*, August 2, 2018, https://www.bbc.co.uk/bbcthree/article/f1d7fed0-4ddf-4a8a-94b9-ea05f913cdd2.
[4] B. J. Bethel, 'Young men search for answers, rising star Jordan Peterson gives them', *The Sydney Morning Herald*, February 23, 2018, https://www.smh.com.au/world/north-america/young-men-search-for-answers-rising-star-jordan-peterson-gives-them-20180223-p4z1cw.html.
[5] Sam Woolfe, 'Why Does Jordan Peterson Appeal to So Many Young Men?', *Blake Writes for the Modern Man,* September 14, 2018, https://www.blakewrites.com/articles/why-does-jordan-peterson-appeal-to-so-many-young-men.
[6] Bryant, 'Why do young men worship Professor Jordan Peterson?',
[7] '12 Rules for Life by Jordan Peterson', *Nateliason* (blog), accessed November 19, 2019, https://www.nateliason.com/notes/12-rules-for-life-jordan-peterson.
[8] Nancy Pearcy, *Total Truth: Liberating Christianity from Its Cultural Captivity*, (Wheaton, IL: Crossway, 2005), 253.
[9] Jeremy Boreing, 'Daily Wire Backstage: Live in Long Beach', Daily Wire (YouTube) August 22, 2019, https://www.youtube.com/watch?v=EAbuWCWv8kE.
[10] Pearcy, 270.
[11] Pearcy, 274.
[12] Luke Kinsella, 'Jordan Peterson is preaching to a generation desperate to grow up', *News.com.au*, March 22, 2018, https://www.news.com.au/lifestyle/health/mind/jordan-peterson-is-preaching-to-a-generation-desperate-to-grow-up/news-story/c1996c25c093450c7aad68000f9d0101.
[13] 'Frontline of Free Speech (LIVE) | Jordan Peterson & Ben Shapiro | POLITICS', Rubin Report, YouTube, January 31, 2018, https://youtu.be/1opHWsHr798.
[14] Marty Nemko PhD, 'The Peter Pan Syndrome: Why smart people fail', *Psychology Today*, May 13, 2016, https://www.psychologytoday.com/au/blog/how-do-life/201605/the-peter-pan-syndrome.
[15] 'Face the Dragon and Get the Gold', Wisdom Talks, YouTube, March 14, 2019, https://www.youtube.com/watch?v=VX8ttxTPjhA.

LOST BOYS

[16] 'Jordan Peterson and Ben Shapiro: Religion, Trans Activism, and Censorship', Ruben Report, YouTube, November 18, 2018,
https://www.youtube.com/watch?time_continue=2&v=1opHWsHr798&feature=emb_logo

[17] 'Answer the call to adventure and go into the unknown – Wisdom from Jordan Peterson', Wisdom Lover, YouTube, January 31, 2018,
https://www.youtube.com/watch?v=OYq-NpHMOVw.

Peter Pan and Ecstasies Innumerable

— 8 —

Forget them, Wendy. Forget them all. Come with me where you'll never, never have to worry about grown-up things again.

– J. M. Barrie, *Peter Pan*

FOLLOWING ON FROM THE PREVIOUS CHAPTER where I introduced Jordan Peterson, let me take you on a brief diversion—but a necessary one. It will most likely take you down memory lane of childhood fairytales, and in doing so will give you a new perspective on understanding our lost boys.

Even though the childhood classic story of *Peter Pan*[1] was popular with children, as a child I always saw it as a scary story about children being pursued by an evil man and a dangerous crocodile who could bite off limbs.

Listening to a Jordan Peterson lecture, I was captivated by his explanation of the story and how he compared the fictional character of Peter Pan with today's young men. I was so intrigued by what he said that I bought the original *Peter Pan* book and read it with great interest. As we know, there is much more in a book than a movie. I read it once, then a few times more. I was *hooked*.

Before sharing what I learned, I need to give you an explanation of *archetypes*, as it's not in our everyday vocabulary, and you need to understand it to get the gist of Peterson's message. Archetypes are patterns of universally shared knowledge about behaviours, people, and personalities that every person in society is believed to know innately.[2] For instance, a mother reads a story to young child, the child seems to subconsciously know who the hero is, how heroes should act, who the bad guy is, what bad guys tend to do, and so on. Parents don't spend time explaining, 'Now this is the bad guy because he is doing such and such.' The child just seems to know.

So, back to Pan. For those who are not familiar, here is a brief overview of the story to spark your memory.

Peter Pan is a boy who not only never grew up but outrightly refused to grow up. Three children from a loving family, Wendy, John, and Michael, are taken to Neverland by Peter Pan and his fairy companion, Tinker Bell.

Peter Pan and Ecstasies Innumerable

Neverland is an island reached by flight, full of adventures with pirates, Indians, and wild animals. Pan is the captain of a band of Lost Boys—children who apparently fell out of their prams as babies while their nannies or caretakers were not looking. Yes, really. Captain Hook is Peter's sworn enemy, who lost an arm when Peter fed it to a crocodile during a fight. This crocodile, who also swallowed a clock, continually pursues Captain Hook as Hook pursues Peter. The tick-tock sound coming from the belly of the crocodile is an ominous early warning sign to Hook whenever the crocodile comes near. Hook is afraid of the day when the ticking will inevitably stop, when the clock runs out and the crocodile will be able to take him by surprise.

The children have one exciting adventure after another on the island of Neverland. Wendy becomes a mother figure to the Lost Boys, who live with Peter in a secret hideaway under the ground. The Lost Boys are truly lost and long for a mother and family. They don't remember their real families and are convinced by Pan that their real mothers have forgotten about them. Wendy believes that her mother, Mrs. Darling, would be missing her children and would always leave the window open, even in winter, so they could fly back home. Peter, a narcissist, doesn't want anyone to leave, so he continually attempts to destroy their hope by convincing the Lost Boys that their mothers have closed the window and forgotten about

LOST BOYS

them. He tries to deceive Wendy and her brothers as well, but they remain strong in their hope.

Tinker Bell is a strange character. She is Peter's fairy, and a 'common' one at that. She is often rude and insulting. She has an intense enmity and jealously toward Wendy and attempts to kill her twice in the story. She also has a loyal side as she sacrificed her life to save Peter by drinking the deadly poison meant for him. Fairies die when children stop believing in them, so their lives are tenuous.

The story peaks when Peter rescues Wendy, her brothers, and the Lost Boys, who were kidnapped by Hook and his band of pirates. As they are about to walk the plank, Peter makes a dramatic entry, frees his companions, kills the pirates, and makes Hook walk the plank, where he is consumed by the crocodile. Reluctantly, Peter and Tinker Bell then escort Wendy and her brothers, together with the Lost Boys, back home. Mischievous Peter flies ahead with Tinker Bell to Wendy's home to close the window before they get there to prove that their parents have forgotten them so they will return to Neverland. When Peter arrives, he finds the window open and Mrs. Darling in the children's nursery sitting by the piano asleep. She had been playing the piano and weeping for her children, as she has done every night since they left. Peter notices the tear on her cheek. He, too, is moved and, in his hesitation,

Peter Pan and Ecstasies Innumerable

does not close the window in time before the children arrive.

Mr. and Mrs. Darling are overjoyed at the return of their children, and they agree to adopt the Lost Boys. Wendy and Mrs. Darling try to convince Peter to come inside and join their family too. Although Peter is pulled by a longing for the warmth of a family, he rejects the offer. The saddest part of the story is the image of Peter alone, a Lost Boy himself, looking forlornly through the window at the warmth of a happy family inside. He is not just *unwilling* but *unable* to enter.

> There could not have been a lovelier sight; but there was none to see it except a little boy who was staring in at the window. He had ecstasies innumerable that other children can never know; but he was looking through the window at the one joy from which he must be forever barred.[3] — J. M. Barrie, Peter Pan

The story continues with Wendy given permission to travel with Peter back to Neverland each year to help with his spring cleaning. Wendy is ready every spring break, but sometimes Peter doesn't turn up and misses a year. He doesn't remember the old adventures; he doesn't even remember Tinker Bell. When Wendy enquires about Tinker Bell, Peter has no memory of the fairy and says that he has had so many fairies that he can't really remember them individually. Wendy is mortified. The story ends in the future, where Wendy is married with her own daughter. She is sitting in the same nursery, watching her child sleep, when Peter alights in the room. Peter is expecting Wendy to come with him for spring break, but she has to explain to him that she has grown up and is a mother herself. The cycle then continues with Wendy's daughter and so on down the generations. Peter remains an eternal boy.

Now back to the archetypes.

According to Peterson, the original *Peter Pan* story has some significant archetypes.[4] He explains that when children reach adolescence, they want to shed their childish ways and grow up. The thought of growing up to Peter Pan is horrifying. Wendy is a real girl, and Peter is unable to establish a true relationship with her because he refuses to mature, thereby sacrificing a real connection. Wendy wants to grow up like any normal girl, get married, have kids, and have a life of her own. She accepts her mortality and her maturity. In contrast, Peter Pan has a *sort* of relationship with a fairy called Tinker Bell, who is not real, perhaps a figure of his imagination. Peterson suggests that in today's culture, Tinker Bell is like the 'fairy of pornography' representing fantasy relationships with girls and a substitute for the real thing.[5]

In addition, Peterson talks about authority figures. The only adult in Peter's life is an evil pirate who Peter hates. He's a tyrant, he's brutal, and he's a coward. The crocodile represents death or time, and time has already gotten a piece of Captain Hook and is pursuing him for more, until it finally takes him at the end of the story. All adults must accept that they are finite and limited, and if they cannot accept that, then they can become tyrants and try to control everything around them. Peter does not want to end up as Captain Hook, his only role model.

Peterson is harsh on the Lost Boys, saying that they are basically a bunch of losers and it is not a great accomplishment to be their leader. If a child does not shed their childhood potential and grow up, he will remain a Lost Boy, 'a 40-year-old Lost Boy, which is a horrifying thing to behold. It's almost as if you are the corpse of a child, the living corpse of a child. Because who the hell wants a 6-year-old 40-year-old? You're a little on the stale side by that point, not the world's happiest individual'.[6]

Indeed, we have a phenomenon of Lost Boys who have ecstasies innumerable but deep down long for that which they believe they have been forever barred.

---

[1] Written first as a play produced in 1904.
[2] Kendra Cherry, 'The 4 Major Jungian Archetypes', *verywell mind*, updated September 12, 2019, https://www.verywellmind.com/what-are-jungs-4-major-archetypes-2795439.
[3] J. M. Barrie, *Peter Pan* (1911; repr., New York: Penguin Books, 2004), 141.
[4] 'Jordan Peterson – Peter Pan, King of the Losers', January 21, 2018, YouTube, https://www.youtube.com/watch?v=zp9igXSEgUc.
[5] 'Jordan Peterson explaining Peter Pan and how not to become him', *Reality Talk Reviews,* YouTube, August 9, 2017,
https://www.youtube.com/watch?v=SGGIN3nQ5kQ.
[6] 'Jordan B Peterson - Peter Pan As Wasted Potential', *Ander Lewis*, YouTube, February 2, 2017, https://www.youtube.com/watch?v=AqCzsw6LyjA.

Counterinsurgency

Fighting Back

— 9 —

The truth is far more powerful than any weapon of mass destruction.

– Mahatma Gandhi

OUR WESTERN CIVILISATION was built upon the values of the Judeo-Christian worldview. The freedom and prosperity that Western nations have enjoyed is because we have the highest freedom and wealth indices in the world. However, since the cultural revolutions of the '60s and '70s, an insurgency of Marxist ideology has swept through the channels of our education system, news media, and entertainment, otherwise known as the *establishment*. This is the new accepted orthodoxy.

LOST BOYS

Our children are subjected to this ideological indoctrination through the National Curriculum, which has been described in an IPA report to the government as 'unbalanced, biased, and fundamentally hostile to Australia's Western Civilisation legacy'.[1] In addition, our universities are also teaching and encouraging hostility toward the values we hold as Australians.[2] Many in older generations have been shocked by the anger and distain many young people emerging from our universities hold for our nation and our history. We are producing citizens who detest their own nation and despise those who attempt to honour our past. Hence the opposition to Australia Day celebrations and the dishonouring of other significant national days such as ANZAC Day. In addition, Christianity, the religion that provided the values our great nation was built on, has been booted out of schools and trodden underfoot and the very words of Scripture labelled as offensive 'hate speech'.

A note needs to be inserted here to understand this and the next chapters. Over the last few decades there has been a trend for Christians to totally disengage from what is going on politically, and this has been detrimental to Western society. Politics is influenced by culture, and culture is shaped by our worldview. For instance, to use a common example, if the culture believes that life is sacred and begins at conception, then citizens will vote for the political party that upholds this worldview, who will create policies that preserve the life of the unborn. If the culture believes that life begins after the womb and a woman is free to take the life of her unborn, then the citizens will vote for a political party that upholds this view and which develop policies that support this position. And the same goes for any issue, whether it is in regard to free speech, immigration, what constitutes marriage, the size of the military, foreign policy, free markets, and so on. Good ideas help society to flourish. If Christians do not engage intelligently in the public square of ideas, then it is to the detriment of society, as opposing ideas will win the day.

The good news is that there is an active counterinsurgency movement that's already engaged on a new battlefront.

Young Christians are on the frontlines debating ideas more than ever, and they are making an impact. I believe that many in older generations have no idea this is happening. The reason? The battle for young people's minds is now being fought in cyberspace, a place where many older people have not been or perhaps dare not go. It's a new public square where young people are challenging each other with alternative views from what has become mainstream. They are debating ideas and opinions that the mainstream media are not engaging or are only providing a one-sided view.

To illustrate, let me share Molly's story. I tell this story because I have watched closely Molly's journey, and hers is typical. However, I believe that most young people who have travelled this similar path are young men, as I've already touched on and will explain further in the next chapters.

Recently as I sat in a cinema waiting for the film to begin, a young man sitting in front of me was scrolling through his social media on his smartphone. I recognised some of the posts he was viewing as those giving a counter-narrative to the establishment, not unlike the ones that Molly has been following. Here's her story:

Molly graduated Year 12 as dux in 2018 and is now studying at one of Australia's top universities. She is from an average home with a mum and dad and two siblings. Her parents have always held a somewhat negative view of religion, particularly Christianity, believing it to be a form of mass mind control. This same negative view has been continually reinforced through her public education experience.

I remember a discussion a few years ago around our dinner table when Molly strongly defended abortion as a 'woman's right'. Her arguments were the typical ones she had been fed from the establishment. In the ensuing years, there were many such friendly debates between Molly and the young adults in our family. Molly really enjoyed being challenged, as she loves debating and has a rational mind. Normally, at school when she debated, she could easily win; however, she was finding that her nihilistic arguments didn't stack up in an intellectual debate outside of her normal circles.

The continual challenging of her acquired views and her inability to defend her stand led Molly to think that perhaps she needed to do some research. She came across various young YouTubers and began listening to alternative views on a range of social and political issues. I interviewed her about her current stance on abortion and other topics, and this is what she said:

> I've changed my views on many things in the last six months. Firstly, I've changed my views on religion. I have always been against religion. I was against religion because it was the only attitude I ever had. I never really thought about it other than when it was mentioned by my family in a negative way. Now that I'm not spending time at school and with my family all of the time, it has given me some distance to think for myself. … I think my original views are easier to live by rather than to live by God's moral code. It's scary to have to live by a moral code. … I just want to be comfortable with where I'm at. … I adapted to the only views that I was surrounded with. To live my own way is a lot less confronting and a lot easier than feeling like I have a moral judgement over my shoulder.
>
> At school in Year 11 and 12, our English teacher introduced us to social and political topics from a very left-leaning perspective and did not give us any alternative viewpoints. We had to watch a video by Michael Moore, who I've since discovered is a radical socialist. And gender roles of male and female, I was

taught that they were evil, but I now believe that men and women are different and can do some things better and some things not as great. I thought I can be the same as a man and I shouldn't have to live by gender roles. I remember when we studied The Crucible, which is an analogy of the Red Scare or the infiltration of communism during the Cold War times. Our teacher told us that communism was just another ideology like our capitalist democracy. Stalinism in history is totally different to what I was being taught in Year 12.

Looking back now, I would have debated my teacher more. I've discovered that all my arguments had come from a sense of misguided compassion. When you educate yourself, what is really compassionate is more conservative ideas; they work, and they lift people up. When I think back about school, it shaped and confirmed my original social and political ideas. At university it's the same in that it just confirms those views that I grew up with and was taught in school. I don't agree with all the views of my university professors, but I don't say anything. No one challenges a university professor.

In regard to my view on abortion, after having the debates with your family, I went and did research. I remember watching a YouTube video on abortion by Allie Beth Stuckey called 'Abortion Ain't Biblical',[3] and it was really, really interesting because I had never heard abortion described like that and it was heartbreaking ... and the proof that what is in a woman's womb is a human being. There is no denying that life has inherent value, like why do I value my own life, why do I value others' lives, why do we interact this way? Why are we us? The universe points to divine design. It's really frightening how kids come out of the education system as a product of the education system's agenda. I think back on how I thought abortion was okay, and I feel really bad.

In my previous book I interviewed Molly and asked her questions about where we come from and our purpose in life and where we are going when we die. I read her answers back to her:

Where do we come from?

The stars. The stars are made up of atoms, and humans are made up of atoms. All atoms come from stars originally.

Why are we here?

There is no purpose as such. We are here to make our own purpose.

What is right and wrong?

I don't know. I think it is what we have been taught by our parents. Our parents were taught by their parents and so on, down the line. This stems originally from some genuinely good people who passed lessons down through the ages. Right and wrong is changeable.

Where do we go when we die?

I don't know, but I think there is a strong possibility that there is an afterlife. I don't really want there to be an afterlife.

LOST BOYS

> Why?
>
> Because I would rather just live a good life and die and then have no consciousness anymore.[4]

Molly looked perturbed as I read to her. She said that listening to what she thought back then makes her feel really sad. She no longer holds those views. She believes that we have been divinely created for a purpose. She is still working all of this out, recognising that she is on a journey to seek truth and has since started attending a church.

Jesus was a counterinsurgent, challenging the insurgent views introduced by the religious and cultural leaders, helping the Jews to reconnect with their God and to understand what true religion was. His closest companions were continually confronted with Jesus going against the culture and religious system. During His ministry years, He challenged them constantly about their accepted norms. He confronted them on things like attitudes toward women and children, caring for the poor, using the temple as a marketplace, feelings about the sick and unclean, healing on the Sabbath, adultery, public giving, who is the greatest, and the list goes on. It seems as though a lot of boulders in their path to believing needed to be confronted with truth and removed to make a clear way for the gospel. Just like Molly's.

[1] Stephanie Forrest, 'Submission to Department of Education Review of the National Curriculum', Institute of Public Affairs, March 2014, https://ipa.org.au/wp-content/uploads/archive/IPA_Submission-National_Curriculum_Review-March_2014.pdf.

[2] Matthew Lesh, 'Is it Monash or Marxist University?', Institute of Public Affairs, April 3, 2018, https://ipa.org.au/publications-ipa/is-it-monash-or-marxist-university.

[3] Allie B. Stuckey, 'Ep 46 Relatable: Abortion Ain't Biblical', Blaze TV, October 16, 2018, https://www.blazetv.com/video/ep-72--relatable-abortion-aint-biblical--allie.

[4] Cindy McGarvie, *#JesusRevolution: Real and Radical* (Youth for Christ Australia 2018), 75.

A New Battlefront

— 10 —

We destroy every proud obstacle that keeps people from knowing God.

– 2 Corinthians 10:5 NLT

THIS CHAPTER NEEDS TO BE PREFACED with some information to set the scene. A new battlefront has opened up. It's not the only battlefront, but it is significant and must be understood. According to McCrindle researchers, those born from 1995–2009 are known as Generation Z, or Gen Z, iGens, Generation Connected, Screenagers, dot.com kids, the Zeds, and Digital Integrators. The upcoming generation, Gen Alpha, born since 2010, are known as Up Agers, Generation Glass (from looking at screens), Global Gen, and Multi Models.[1] As you can see by these titles, our young people are globally connected through the internet. Social media has blown up and has become a platform for sharing the good, the bad, and the ugly. Whether we like it or not, this has become a battlefront that young people are engaging more and more.

I have spent hundreds of hours over the last twenty-four months following YouTubers, mostly Millennials, mostly from the US, and mostly Christian. I've watched their videos, which consist of reporting and discussing current issues and interviewing of people on the street, at protests, or at rallies. I've consistently read their posts on Instagram and listened to their podcasts. These young YouTubers are extremely active in the new public square discussing social and political issues outside of mainstream media. They are very smart, perceptive, and incredibly brave. They speak the language of this generation, sometimes rather offensive to the older Gens. Sometimes they make mistakes and can be too divisive, but often they are on point. They don't hold back on boldly presenting a Christian worldview. They don't force their beliefs on anyone but intelligently and unashamedly present a different perspective on social and political issues. This viewpoint is distinctly different from the nihilistic, biased media and the orthodoxy taught at universities.

When one challenges social issues and discusses ideas about how humans can flourish, then it automatically becomes political, and Christians don't like going there. Politics has a bad reputation of power and corruption. My

A New Battlefront

point is that we must engage in the battlefield of ideas, particularly discussing what has now become orthodoxy or generally accepted views, and not shy away from tackling them.

It's important to explain briefly the new orthodoxy and how it is being socially engineered. There is a new term floating around the media: to be *woke*. It's a word which describes those who are alert to detecting offences such as forms of aggression, oppressions, and injustices like 'male privilege' or 'white privilege', cultural appropriation, and so on. To be woke means you are more perceptive or have been awakened to identifying offences perpetrated by others and can call them out—and many times, punish them publicly through social media. It's 'cool' to be woke; most of Hollywood is woke. If you are not woke, then it is highly likely you are perceived as bigoted, racist, ignorant, and privileged, an oppressor of sorts. This new 'religion' of the woke people, who are mostly Millennials, together with the media class and those in higher education institutions, keep society in check so that everyone tows the line, agrees with their worldview, and abides by its continually changing rules.

The Australian education system's National Curriculum and universities have included the woke ideology of gender, race, and equality into learning to ensure that the new generation is all familiar and can follow the rules without questioning them.[2] Even our national broadcaster has become a proponent of the preachy and virtuous woke culture.

This is disturbing social engineering.

The woke belief system is an ideological boulder that prevents young people from challenging ideas and behaviours that might normally be contested —even incredibly dumb ideas.

In addition, young, idealistic people who genuinely care about others and their world can be deceived into self-idolatry or self-righteousness, for being woke is about greatly admiring one's own kindness, compassion, and virtue. It's signaling one's own righteousness and goodness to others whilst actively calling out—often in the most intolerant of ways—and persecuting those who transgress. It's quite pharisaical, actually, and you can see why young people, particularly young men, are looking elsewhere for better ideas.

Peter Hitchens commented quite accurately on this woke attitude that 'belief in one's own virtue makes dialogue impossible' and 'if you think your opponent is bad, not just wrong, then why should you listen to them?'[3]

Research released in 2019 by the Institute of Public Affairs in Australia found that 56 percent of male university students feel more comfortable expressing their views on social media, with 65 percent of young men saying that they are exposed to more new ideas on social media. Young men at university are self-censoring in an

A New Battlefront

institution that should welcome the open discussion of ideas. Janet Albrechtsen wrote about this phenomenon:

> Young male students are disproportionately looking elsewhere for a more diverse range of opinions, and for a space where they can express their own views. ... The terrific news is that students don't have short concentration spans when they are listening to views that challenge the orthodoxy. ... This survey shows that they are hungry for ideas.[4]

You may be asking, 'How does this relate to this new battleground of cyber warfare?'

The young men and women leading the charge on social media are using cyber warfare to remove the ideological boulders or lies that have been carefully put in place to keep them from receiving and accepting truth. One of the strategies of stifling truth is by removing history and civics from the education system as a foundation to understanding who we are. Young people in the West don't know the biblical origins of the constitutional freedoms they enjoy today or the biblical origins of our law system, and have been fed an historical counter-narrative that distorts truth.

So if young people are fighting back through social media, what does that look like?

It's videos posted on YouTube, Facebook, and Instagram, as well as other platforms, debunking the nihilistic and Marxist ideology and the woke commandments. It's edgy posts and memes on Facebook, Instagram, Twitter, and

LOST BOYS

other platforms. And don't underestimate YouTube videos:

- Almost half of the world's internet users are on YouTube.
- YouTube is home to 50 million content creators.
- Millennials prefer YouTube twice as much as traditional TV. [5]

No wonder 75 percent of children dream of becoming YouTubers![6]

Just ask a child, particularly a boy of around 8 to 12 years, who his favourite YouTuber is, and see how his face lights up.

So, if social media is a new battle terrain, and young men are flocking there to listen to ideas and opinions as well as to share their own, who are they listening to for thoughts and views to help them understand what's going on in our world?

One of the names I constantly hear amongst young men is Ben Shapiro. Ben is an orthodox Jew, who graduated from high school at sixteen and went on to graduate from Harvard Law School. As a seventeen-year-old he was writing a column for a newspaper, and by the time he was twenty-one, he had already written two books. In 2015, he cofounded the media company *The Daily Wire*, and his daily podcast, 'The Ben Shapiro Show', is the top conservative podcast in the USA, with millions of subscribers. He has written several books, including a best seller titled *The Right Side of History: How Reason and Moral Purpose Made the West Great*. Ben is a social and political commentator and a strong advocate against the woke ideology, advocating for things like free speech, free markets, freedom of religion, and strong families and marriage and for the life of the unborn. He is often invited by conservative groups at universities to give talks. His fact and logic discussions and arguments are powerful, enlightening, and highly respected by a growing number of young people.

And fact and logic are vital for young people, particularly young men who want to be intellectually engaged, as we have previously discussed. Being raised in a highly feminised society, where popular discourse and important decisions made by societal leaders seem to be feeling-based and, therefore, more and more relative, has meant they are looking for other platforms to exchange ideas freely.

Charlie Kirk is another incredibly bright and articulate young YouTuber. He founded an organisation called Turning Point USA when he was eighteen. He's now an accomplished author and speaker with regular appearances on television commenting on social and political topics. Also, his videos garner hundreds of thousands of views each week on social media platorms. He is open about his Christian faith and speaks with confidence and intelligence that commands respect. When asked on a YouTube interview about his faith, he said this:

> I believe in a God. I believe in the Bible, the greatest book ever to exist with five thousand years of history, over 34 authors and 66 books. I believe God came in human form. ... God came down as a gift for us broken humans. ... To be able to accept this gift, Jesus Christ, ... Jesus Christ was God in flesh, ... we have to realise that there is something bigger than ourselves. ... [Those who believe and observe Scripture] approach life in a much different way, maybe my opinion and what I do is not the most important in the world.[7]

I encourage you to view the complete interview, which has hundreds of thousands of views, as it gives an excellent example of the caliber of young people in the public square debating ideas in a logical and thoughtful manner.

One of the brightest and most articulate young thinkers in Australia's public square today is Martyn Iles, the managing director of the Australian Christian Lobby. He has taken to social media with his program, *The Truth of It*, a weekly look at Australian politics through a Christian worldview. He unashamedly advocates for truth and is an example of both courage and valor as he navigates the constant hostility of mainstream media and those who advocate for tolerance yet do not practice it. We need more like him.

As I pen this book, Kanye West, an American Grammy Award winning rapper and record producer, announced publicly his conversion to the Christian faith.[8] Although it's great to see amazing conversions like this, it will be a difficult journey navigating his newfound faith in the public domain. That said, Kanye has been outspoken on social media, condemning things like the woke ideology of victimhood, the welfare state, and many other issues including the high abortion rate among black Americans. It's interesting that he has immediately begun to engage in the public square to confront the social and political issues he believes are opposed to the flourishing of his fellow black Americans. He has even disclosed that he has been battling a sex and porn addiction that began at age five when he found a *Playboy* magazine belonging to his father. Reports have stated that since Kanye's public announcement of his conversion there has been increased interest in Christianity, with Google searches spiking about "Jesus" and "What Christians believe?" since he released his album *Jesus Is King*.[9] In addition, the American Bible Society gave away in less than two weeks 8,800 bibles to Kanye West fans 'who are hungry to learn about God'.[10]

But I digress.

To re-emphasise my previous point, young people, particularly young men, are engaging by the score in a new public square contesting and debating ideas they are not freely able to do in the mainstream education system or media. Many are changing their opinions on God, justice, freedoms, government, life, culture, and much more because of the discussion of these ideas. It is speaking their language, explaining logical answers to life's big questions.

I believe that on this battlefront young people are demolishing arguments and pretensions set up against the knowledge of God, pretensions that have given young people a narrative that there is no Creator, purpose, nor moral code to live by and that life has no value.

Young men *want* to discuss, debate, and contest their ideas and listen to new perspectives. They *want* to engage their intellect. The iGens, or Generation Connected, are active in the public square of an international cyber-community along with their predecessors, Gen Ys, who are just as globally connected.

Watch out for the upcoming Gen Alphas, the Generation Glass, who knows what's ahead for them.

---

[1] 'Gen Z and Gen Alpha Infographic Update', *McCrindle*, accessed November 16, 2019, https://mccrindle.com.au/insights/blogarchive/gen-z-and-gen-alpha-infographic-update.

[2] For more information on what is being taught at universities read *'The Coddling of the American Mind: How Good Intentions and Bad Ideas Are Setting Up a Generation for Failure* by Greg Lukianoff and Jonathan Haidt (New York: Penguin, 2018).

[3] 'Conversations with John Anderson: Featuring Peter Hitchens (Part I)' January 13, 2019, https://www.youtube.com/watch?v=V7K1A8jgF1w

[4] Janet Albrechtsen, 'University Fail', *The Weekend Australian Inquirer*, August 31-September 1, 2019, 31.

[5] '10 Best YouTube User Statistics for Marketers', Media Kix, accessed November 16, 2019, https://mediakix.com/blog/youtube-user-statistics-demographics-for-marketers.

⁶ '10 Best YouTube User Statistics',
⁷ 'The Candace Owens Show: Charlie Kirk', *Prager U*, May 5, 2019, https://www.youtube.com/watch?v=Fle4Qn9fCGs.
⁸ Biography.com, 'Editors, Kanye West Biography', *A&E Television Networks*, updated October 27, 2019, https://www.biography.com/musician/kanye-west.
⁹ Caldron Pool, 'Huge spike in searches about Christianity after the release of "Jesus Is King"', The Caldron Pool, November 4, 2019, https://caldronpool.com/huge-spike-in-searches-about-christianity-after-the-release-of-jesus-is-king.
¹⁰ CBN News, 'American Bible Society Gives 8,800 Free Bibles to Kanye West Fans Hungry to Learn About God', *CBN News*, November 12, 2019, https://www1.cbn.com/cbnnews/entertainment/2019/november/american-bible-society-gives-thousands-of-free-bibles-to-kanye-west-fans-hungry-to-learn-about-god.

And That's How It's Done

Insights into Spiritual Warfare

— 11 —

It is funny how mortals always picture us as putting things into their minds: in reality our best work is done by keeping things out.

– C. S. Lewis, *The Screwtape Letters*

IT WAS INTRIGUING TO READ ABOUT and watch the live footage of how the infamous ISIS leader Abu

LOST BOYS

Bakr al-Baghdadi was taken out. The amount of intelligence gathering to find him and narrow down his location was phenomenal. The mission involved raiding a compound outside a village in Syria and included eight twin-rotor Chinook helicopters flying over Turkey airspace at night, supported by unmanned military aircraft and ships, commandos with dogs, and a military robot. The gate of the compound was booby-trapped and needed to be breached before the highly trained Delta-force soldiers could even enter the compound. The use of infrared and satellite imagery led to the pursuit of the enemy in an underground tunnel system. After the operation, the work continued, with collecting intelligence, DNA testing to identify the body of the enemy leader, and so on.[1]

What if the American government recruited off the street some enthusiastic, willing, fit young men, cut their hair, put a uniform on them, put a gun in their hand with some ammunition, gave them some other specialised equipment, and loaded them onto the CH-47 military helicopters to take out the ISIS leader? The mission could not be executed without *trained* and *disciplined* soldiers, no matter how much specialised weaponry or support systems they had or how enthusiastic the new recruits.

Likewise, spiritual warfare cannot happen without training, as I've highlighted in previous chapters. Soldiers are then ready for battle to execute effective missions and to stand against attack.

And That's How It's Done

Often when we think of spiritual warfare, it conjures up images of driving out demons or such. However, spiritual warfare is broader than that. It's something we as Christian warriors practice daily in our *normal Christian lives*, whether on behalf of ourselves or for others.

To illustrate just how normal it is to take down a giant in one's life, I've penned the following story of one of my victories over a personal stronghold. Taking down strongholds is spiritual warfare in practice, and we've all been given the weapons to do it. We just need to learn to use them.

During my childhood I struggled with jealousy. I was jealous of my sister, relatives, friends, and anyone else who happened to have something I wanted. Jealousy was so much a part of me that I thought it was something everyone battled with and a normal, acceptable thing I would just have to put up with for the rest of my life. It caused me much unhappiness and discontent and was often the cause of conflicts as my jealousy even drove me to a point of hating others. I had an inability to celebrate good things that happened to those around me. As I grew into adulthood, I developed techniques to hide my jealousy. I don't think people would have described me as a jealous person, but on the inside, I was often crippled with it.

Just before I turned twenty-one, I chose to follow Christ and was radically transformed. John Wesley's hymn describes my experience well:

> Long my imprisoned spirit lay
> Fast bound in sin and nature's night;
> Thine eye diffused a quick'ning ray,
> I woke, the dungeon flamed with light;
> My chains fell off, my heart was free;
> I rose, went forth and followed Thee.[2]

I experienced incredible freedom and release and vowed to follow my Saviour for the rest of my days.

Fast forward ten years. I was a young mother, serving with my husband on the mission field of Africa. I found myself at a point of total defeat. I felt like a fake Christian. On the outside I seemed full of faith and was honoured as a missionary, and yet I was still struggling to overcome besetting sins, destructive behavioural patterns, and self-centredness.

In light of what I discussed in the first chapter about the Israelites taking the promised land, my situation was similar. I had moved into the promised land but failed to learn the art of warfare to fully take the ground that had been promised —some strongholds were still to be taken—and to keep the ground that I had won.

One day I was sitting on a swing under a huge tree watching my young sons playing in the red African dirt. I was lamenting the state of my heart, not seeing any victory or power in my life. I cried out to God, 'What is wrong with me?!' Immediately the thought came to my mind from Proverbs 15:11 where it explains that even hell holds no secrets from God, so how much more would he know the

And That's How It's Done

human heart? How much more does He know *my* heart? Suddenly I really believed that God knew my heart. I knew He could see my problems and brokenness and that He'd lead me to freedom. I was stuck, and He would sort it out. Thus began an exciting journey of growth, learning the Word of God and standing firm in the truth of who God says He is and who God says I am.

I began to pray Scripture and study the Bible intensely. I also learned to be alert and expose wrong feelings by asking myself, 'What is that feeling you have in your heart right now?' One day I found myself disingenuously expressing happiness for someone who had experienced something good, and immediately I caught that thought, went to my room, and examined it under the Light. I was shocked that it was envy. Could this be true?

I then researched *envy* and *jealousy*, as they appeared to be the same. However, I was stunned at what I discovered. I learned that envy is far more odious, much more wicked, than jealousy. They both belong to the family of coveting and idolatry. Jealousy sees something it wants and desires it; envy sees something it wants and not only desires it but does not want the person who owns it to have it either. There is a sense of malice in envy. When I saw what it was, how destructive it had been in my life, and learned it was a form of idolatry, I hated it and repented. It was like I just discovered I was holding some germ-ridden, contaminated thing, and when I realised what it was, threw it off in disgust and washed my hands of it.

I didn't realise how bound up and controlled I had been from envy until I was free. For the next several weeks, the feeling of envy would pop up, and I would immediately recognise it in repulsion and tell it to get lost. Over the months it became less and less until it vanished. It's now been so long that it's hard to remember what it felt like to be gripped by envy.

Our Boys Can Break Free

I have interviewed a lot of young men who have been gripped by the stronghold of porn addiction and have used the powerful spiritual weapons available to us to break free. Each story is different. Some overcame quickly, while others needed support through the process from their family or Christian community, including counsellors, who are also God's providence to us as we fight battles. The encouraging message is that our boys and men can break free. I've shared just a few of these stories briefly at the end of this chapter.

When we lived in Tanzania, we owned two very large German shepherd guard dogs. One of them we called Simba. He was a huge, black, long-haired Zimbabwean dog the size of a small horse. I have never seen another that size. In fact, when he grew old and passed away, it took four men to move his body. He was extremely strong, and as

And That's How It's Done

you might know, German shepherds are very territorial and will attack other animals that trespass. He had killed other dogs and animals before.

One day as I was reading, I heard some commotion in the backyard and went to investigate. Looking out the back door, I saw Simba fighting another dog who didn't have a chance. Standing a few metres away was my Tanzanian house worker, who had been trying without success to separate them with a broom. She was visibly upset and shaken. Without thinking or even leaving the house—I didn't want to go get my shoes—I commanded Simba to stop and to come around to the front door. He let go of the other dog and simpered off in obedience. I then walked through the house to the front door, opened it, and trapped him inside so that the other dog could be taken away.

It crossed my mind how easy this had been. I had tried to break up Simba's fights before, and even with a few of us, it was extremely difficult and dangerous.

When the coast was clear, I released Simba, went back to my chair, and picked up my book to continue reading. The book I happened to be engrossed in was Neil Anderson's book, *Victory Over the Darkness*. I had been learning about taking authority over evil spirits, because in Africa, witchcraft and spiritism were rife. As I relaxed into reading mode, the words came to my mind, *And that's how it's done.*

LOST BOYS

I was just given a practical lesson on spiritual warfare. I had authority, I was confident in that authority because I knew who I was, and I exercised it without much effort at all.

And that's how it's done.

Charles H. Kraft in his book, *I Give You Authority: Practicing the Authority Jesus Gave Us,* provides some helpful insight into using our authority in spiritual warfare:

> As He [Jesus] set about establishing His kingdom, He assumed the authority (the "glory") He had with the Father before the creation of the world (John 17:5). And because this was occurring behind enemy lines, warfare—spiritual warfare aimed at taking back God's world from the usurper—was inevitable.
>
> He then recruited us to continue the operation in Satan's territory. So the context in which we operate as soldiers in Jesus' army is a context of spiritual warfare. It is on a battlefield that we assume our authority. And it is the enemy of our General Jesus, that we challenge when we exercise that authority. Every time we assert our authority we are cutting into the domain of the imposter king who extorted it from our ancestor Adam. And according to Romans 16:20, it is God's desire that we press on with Jesus until that enemy is crushed under *our* feet.
>
> Our redemption both restores humanity to the possibility of the relationship God intended when he created Adam and Eve and empowers us for victory over the evil one within the territory he stole from

us. Redemption enables both our relationship with God and our victory over Satan. And the authority and power that come with the relationship enable us to participate in present victories over the usurper.[3]

Finally the good part. I end this chapter with three testimonies of young men who have experienced present victories by applying spiritual warfare to slay the giant of porn addiction in their lives. I've changed their names to protect their identities. It's both their hope and mine that these stories will inspire others to go after the freedom that is indeed within their reach.

John's Story

Age: 23

John first saw porn when he followed a pop-up ad while playing games online when he was twelve years old. He clicked the link, and it took him to a porn site. Around the same time, his school friends were getting into it as well on their phones, so they all talked about it and shared pictures and videos. John kept it off his phone until he was fifteen. He estimates that he was totally addicted to porn from ages thirteen to eighteen and lived in constant guilt and shame. He also believed the lie that it would be something he'd always struggle with. When he was fifteen, he heard someone talk about it openly for the first time at a youth group. It helped to be open about it with leaders, but he was still not totally free.

From ages eighteen to twenty-one, John still could not stay away from consuming porn. As he began to walk in his sonship, recognising himself as a child of God, his desire for porn started to weaken. When he was twenty-one, John went to a YFC camp and met some other young guys who were walking free. This gave him the desire to go after freedom even more fiercely, as he could see victory. John says, 'For me the fight of faith is to believe the gospel. What's done is done. I'm now moving forward and experiencing freedom.' John is a natural evangelist, leader and an elite athlete and is currently studying at university.

Nate's Story

Age: 22 years

Nate was first introduced to porn at a friend's house in Grade 5 on their family computer. From then on, they'd watch porn together at each other's houses. Gradually he began to watch porn on his own on the family computer, but when he was issued a school computer in Year 7, he was able to watch porn in his bedroom anytime he wanted, often late at night.

Nate was consuming porn daily from Year 7 to Year 9. It began to lessen a bit when he heard a guy speak about it at his church youth group. It was then he realised that he wasn't the only one struggling, always feeling lonely and isolated. The guy who shared became a mentor to Nate, but being a young guy, he too was still struggling.

And That's How It's Done

As a Christian, Nate says, 'I felt my life was a lie, that I wasn't good enough and was a piece of sh**. Anytime anything came up about forgiving sin, then porn would come up in my mind to condemn me about my double life. I couldn't shake it. I remember my dad coming to me saying multiple times, "I'm proud of you," and I'd cry because I'd think, *How could he be proud of me?*'

Nate was addicted for nine years from an 11-year-old boy to a twenty-year-old young man. He wanted to serve God but was crippled by this stronghold. Nate says, 'I believed that getting free from the addiction was going to take a long time, and that's why it did. But when I understood my righteousness in Christ, it was so quick. When I had a tempting lustful thought, I stood on the belief that that it isn't who I am, and it just left me. Because I recognised that I am righteous, sin is outside my new nature in Christ. Sin is tempting me, [but] I am free from its power.

'There has been a lot of weeping and repenting. It's been funny looking through my journals and seeing how I actually wrote things down from the Bible about my new nature in Christ and how I'm no longer a slave to sin, but now I actually understand it. When I saw others believing it and living it, then I realised it was possible to be free.'

Yes, freedom is possible. Nate is an outdoor wilderness instructor and, on the side, continues to help boys and young men to walk free from porn addiction.

LOST BOYS

Harry's Story

Age: 22 years

Harry was first introduced to porn at the tender age of seven years. He was at a neighbour's house, and the entire family was watching it with all the children around. This traumatised him so much that he struggled with those images constantly, and he never told his parents this dark secret.

From that time on, he began to look at what is called 'soft porn', which for him mainly consisted of looking at sexualised music videos of pop songs on YouTube. Harry recalls, 'I felt dark as a child, mixed with feelings of shame, and I felt dirty, isolated, and alone. Porn made me desperate for connection. I felt a heaviness and wanted people to like me. ... I remember in primary school talking to girls in the playground and having sexual thoughts about them and then withdrawing because of guilt and shame. This led to fear and to withdraw from girls altogether.'

When Harry was in middle school, his Christian school introduced iPads, and from that moment it started what he calls a 'horrific porn addiction', which lasted around five years.

When Harry was fifteen, he went on a Christian youth camp, believed the good news, and was converted to faith in Christ. At that point, he didn't know that consuming porn was wrong, and it wasn't until a year later at the next camp that he heard someone speak about it. When he tried to give it up, he couldn't, particularly since he was consuming porn multiple times per day. He says, 'When I tried to stop, I couldn't sleep and would be exhausted, so I ended up giving in to it. It crippled my fight against it. I couldn't study without it. I felt a lack of control over my life, and I became an angry person. I can't speak of how degrading it is for one's character, as I would wake up in the morning and say *I'm not going to do this*, and by the afternoon, I had done it. It destroys you as a person.'

Even though Harry loved God and wanted to walk in purity, he wasn't able to. He recalls, 'Back in Year 11, I had an encounter with God where I was with my best mate and we were weeping as we were both caught up in this addiction. I turned my Bible to Romans 8:1, where it talks about no condemnation for those in Christ. I thought, *Right, if I'm going to get healed from this, I'm going to read my Bible*, and I started reading my Bible so much, but even after that I still didn't get freedom.

'I was at this time leading Christian youth at school and leading outreach programs and Bible studies, seeing up to thirty to forty kids attending, yet I'd come home and need a sexual release through porn, and that hypocrisy tore me apart. ... I got to the point where I thought I would rather die than be a hypocrite. I lived with my addiction for four to five years, though I was exposed much earlier as a young child.'

LOST BOYS

He continues, 'I told my mum when I was in Year 12. This happened because I started seeing a psychologist for depression. I believe 100 percent my depression was directly related to my porn addiction; it was a defining feature. The Christian psychologist helped me break free. I'd recommend this type of help. The psychologist was able to find clarity of where I needed healing. She helped me to see how I was using porn as a coping mechanism for so many other things. I could go back and recognise that I had used porn to cope in various common situations and in response to certain things in my past. And from those points I could administer the gospel. Learning to recognise those triggers helped me to walk free. Even today I don't keep my phone in my room at night. I put things in place so that I'm not tempted. I'm okay with that.'

The journey to freedom where Harry wasn't relapsing took around fifteen months. When the distances between relapsing got greater, his hope was encouraged, and he could sense freedom and went after it. Harry is now studying theology and is a powerful messenger of the gospel of hope to others.

---

[1] Glen Swan et.al., 'Visual guide to the raid that killed ISIS leader Abu Bakr al-Baghdadi', *The Guardian*, November 1, 2019, https://www.theguardian.com/world/2019/oct/28/visual-guide-to-the-raid-that-killed-isis-leader-abu-bakr-al-baghdadi.
[2] From the hymn 'And Can It Be' by John Wesley.
[3] Charles H. Kraft, *I Give You Authority: Practicing the Authority Jesus Gave Us*, (Minneapolis: Baker Publishing Group) 1997, 26.

Goliath's Dead

— 12 —

The powerful are not as powerful as they seem—
nor the weak as weak.

– Malcolm Gladwell

WHEN HE WAS FIVE YEARS OLD, our eldest son was asked to explain to his Maori uncle about God. His three-year-old younger brother had just thrown out the question, 'Uncle Willie, you don't know the Lord, do you?' They were both standing in the backyard watching him dig a post hole. Mr. Five thought for a while and said gravely, 'Goliath's dead.' The huge hulk of a man was visibly impacted by this profound remark. He shared with others later, 'Two little kids, one said to me, "You don't know the Lord," and the other said, "Your life's dead," and it blew me away!' When their aunt, who'd witnessed the incident, corrected that he had in fact said, 'Goliath's dead', her husband wouldn't accept it, emphasising that he only heard very clearly, 'You don't know the Lord.

LOST BOYS

Your life's dead'. Not long after that he put his faith in Christ.

Goliath's dead. The enemy has been defeated.

The story of David and Goliath is one that we all understand and enjoy. A mighty giant of a warrior with armour and weapons coming against a shepherd boy with nothing but a rudimentary sling and some stones. Although this story is often told as an illustration of defeating giants in our lives, it's also about how God doesn't defeat the enemy using the same methods as the adversary and how God sees the situation from a different perspective.

If you haven't read Malcolm Gladwell's book *David and Goliath: Underdogs, Misfits and the Art of Battling Giants*, then you must.[1] Or if you don't have the time, then listen to his fifteen-minute Ted Talk, 'The Unheard Story of David and Goliath'.[2] Gladwell goes into detail explaining how Goliath, the Philistines' mightiest warrior, was a heavy infantry soldier accustomed to close quarters combat, hence Goliath's armour and modern weaponry of the time—a sword, a spear, and a javelin. Both the Philistines and the Israelites were expecting an Israelite champion to also be a heavy infantry soldier. However, David as a shepherd boy was a marksman with the simple sling. Slingers in ancient armies were part of the artillery and were often the *decisive* factor in defeating the enemy. Gladwell explains that ancient armies were made up of three parts: the cavalry, consisting of horses and chariots;

the heavy infantry foot soldiers; and the artillery, which consisted of archers and slingers.

He goes on to explain that we should not underestimate slingers. The sling was not the Y-shaped instrument some might imagine. It was a long piece of fibre made of wool, hemp, or flax woven together with a pouch in the middle section for placing a stone or projectile. Gladwell explains that the slinger would take the rope at both ends in one hand, whirl the rope with the projectile inside at around six to seven revolutions per second, and release. This projectile travelled at around 35 metres per second, and with the extra-dense barium sulphate stones found around the area, David's projectile was lethal with a stopping power equivalent to a .45 calibre handgun.

In addition, the sling can be deadly accurate, even able to shoot a bird in flight and reach in excess of 400 metres. As a shepherd, David would have spent hours target shooting just like any boy. Imagine hours and hours every day, practicing and getting to the point of trusting your ability to consistently hit the target. David killed a lion and a bear when no one was watching. He may have seemed overconfident for such an untrained soldier, a mere boy with no battle experience, but his ability was lethal.

He picked up five stones, but only used one.

One of the enemy's greatest weapons is 'generating fear' through lies and deception, in essence to bluff.[3] And fear melts hope. The Israelites were gripped with terror, and as they looked at the situation, their hope disintegrated. They were thinking they would have to fight in the same way, hand-to-hand combat. That's why Saul tried to give David his sword and armour. For days the Israelite army were terrorised and tormented over this giant who defied the living God. David had a close relationship with his God and was indignant when he heard the taunts. David won because he knew who he was, what he was capable of, and chose not to play by Goliath's rules.

I remember an incident in Africa with my fellow missionary friend Lauren that illustrates this point.

Lauren, a very petite lady in her early forties from the USA and mother of three, was taking her dog for a walk along the beach with her Tanzanian helper. As they looked ahead, they noticed something a few hundred metres up the beach. It looked like a pack of dogs, maybe about eight of them, attacking a log shape in the shallows. Standing up on the sandbank was a group of onlookers, all men. As they got closer, Lauren realised that the log shape was actually a *person*. Without thinking, she handed the lead of her dog to her companion and took off running toward the dogs screaming commands. As she got close, the dogs scattered and ran off up the beach. A couple of them could not run because their chains were wrapped around the person, who happened to be a man. She ran into the water, freed the dogs, and started dragging the injured man out of the shallows. He was a dead weight and heavy for her. In addition, she had to drop him once or twice to chase off the dogs as they were hanging around maliciously looking to attack again. The men on the sand bank all stood in fear and did not help her until she had dragged the victim up a safe distance from the dogs. Since there were no ambulances, a taxi was called, and Lauren handed the driver money and instructed him to take the man straight to the hospital. The victim had horrific wounds, punctures to his eyes and face, an ear torn off, and was in deep shock. He died shortly after arriving at the hospital.

What a needless death. Fear won the day. Yet this is like a David and Goliath story: a pack of savage dogs, a little woman, and a terrorised group of men.

Gladwell also brings up another interesting point in his book. Goliath most likely had a condition called *acromegaly*, which affects the pituitary gland, causing an overproduction of a growth hormone, hence his giant stature. A side effect of this is double vision and restricted sight. Goliath needed to be led to the position of battle. He also thought David was carrying sticks, maybe from his double vision. The enemy is not as powerful as we might believe.

Many Christians see the adversary as the indestructible terrible giant rather than an enemy that is flawed and can be beaten.

LOST BOYS

One of my favourite books is the classic *The Pilgrim's Progress* by John Bunyan. It's an allegory of a man named Christian and his journey to the Celestial City. At one stage in his journey, he and his companion Hopeful stray from the path and are captured by a giant called Despair and thrown into a dark dungeon. They are deprived of food, water, and light and are repeatedly beaten. Giant Despair gives them some poison and a rope to kill themselves, as he assures them that if they don't do it themselves, then he will tear them apart like he has regularly done to other pilgrims he previously captured. Christian loses hope and decides to take the advice of Giant Despair. The younger Hopeful pleads with him to stay strong. He reminds him of how he has overcome so much already and that their Shepherd will show them a way out. In time, Christian remembers an old key, called Promise, that he has in his pocket, and he uses it to unlock the doors and free both himself and Hopeful. As they unlock the last door, Giant Despair awakens and comes to stop them, but since he has a condition whereby strong sunlight causes him to have seizures, he goes into a fit, and the men are able to escape.

The adversary is not as strong and big as he makes out. Despair is a weapon based on lies that we are too weak and already defeated and that what we are fighting is something beyond our capability. Hopelessness and Giant Despair can be destroyed in the bright light of truth. This battle can be won. Practice using your weapons of warfare like David did, and teach the young generation how to use them. Know who you are and recognise your capabilities in Christ.

The church needs young men who are fully trained for warfare to step up into their God-given calling to slay giants, to pull down strongholds, to build flourishing cities, to protect and provide for their families. Be the hero God has called you to be.

Goliath's dead. Forge forth.

> Then David asked the Lord [when his wives and sons and daughters were carried off], 'Should I chase after this band of raiders? Will I catch them?' And the Lord told him, 'Yes, go after them. You will surely recover everything that was taken from you!'
>
> – 1 Samuel 30:8 NLT

Yes, go after them and *bring them home*.

---

[1] New York: Little, Brown, and Company, 2015.
[2] Malcolm Gladwell, 'The Unheard Story of David and Goliath', *TED Talks*, September 30, 2013, https://www.youtube.com/watch?v=ziGD7vQOwl8.
[3] Jules Gomes, 'David v Goliath 2018 – how Professor P brought Leftie Cathy crashing to earth', *Rebel Priest* (blog), January 25, 2018, https://www.jules-gomes.com/single-post/David-v-Goliath-2018-how-Professor-P-brought-Leftie-Cathy-crashing-to-earth.

A Rally Call to Men

Fear is a reaction. Courage is a decision.

– Sir Winston Churchill

THIS IS A FINAL WORD TO OUR MEN, but there is a particular responsibility to older men. Like the Spartan formations, our older men are the rear guard, encouraging, emboldening, and instructing our young, inexperienced warriors. Too many seem to have abandoned the ranks, leaving our boys vulnerable. Others have gone AWOL and have deserted the battlefield altogether. Some have been conscientious objectors, refusing to acknowledge that it's their battle too, even conceding ground to the enemy to try to appease and avoid conflict. Others have been paralysed and have sat harmlessly in feminised pews. It appears that many of our men don't know how to win anymore.

I have four exhortations I implore you to pursue. If you do, I believe without a doubt that far more than our lost boys will be rescued. Families will be restored, the church will be greatly strengthened, and our culture will be transformed. So here goes.

1. Know your identity in Christ—understand the finished work of Christ; it will transform you!

2. Take up and learn to use your spiritual weapons of warfare, and walk in your God-given authority as a son of our mighty and great commander, God.

3. Start loving the church as Christ does His bride, and change your self-focused outlook. It's your duty to honour and serve the body of Christ on earth to help make it flourish. When the church succeeds, we succeed. When the church is victorious, we are victorious.

4. Get out into the culture and influence change. Be ready to face the spears and daggers that will come when you challenge the current cultural orthodoxies.

> *Rise up, men! We are looking to you. Now is the time for you to lead us in the rescue of our lost boys!*

ABOUT THE AUTHOR

Cindy McGarvie serves as national director of Youth for Christ Australia.

Always one for adventure, Cindy began her career by training as a nurse in the Australian Army, specialising in the operating theatre. After she left the army, she took time out to start a family with her husband, Rod, whom she met in the Australian Defence Force.

After travelling the world with kids in tow, Cindy and Rod felt a calling to the mission field and both trained as Bible translators with Wycliffe Australia. In 1998 they moved to East Africa to serve in a leadership capacity in Uganda for eight years and then Tanzania for four years.

During these years, Cindy discovered an interest and passion for teaching within cultural contexts. As an avid reader with an insatiable curiosity, she began reading prolifically. She took external university courses in history, anthropology, and development.

Upon returning to Australia in 2010, Cindy took on the role of missions director for a local church in Brisbane for a number of years before stepping into the government sector. This fuelled her passion further for culture, politics, and social change. With a desire to serve in Christian ministry again, Cindy was appointed the national director of Youth for Christ Australia in 2015. Missions has always been her strongest passion.

Cindy serves on the board of directors of Wycliffe Australia. In her desire to serve and bring influence within her community, she has been actively involved in her local state high school and served as president of the Parents and Citizens Association for three years until 2019.

Cindy lives with her husband, Rod, in Brisbane. They have five adult children, three sons and two daughters, all forging forth in life's adventures.

Follow

FACEBOOK: www.facebook.com/yfcaustralia/
WEBSITE: www.yfc.org.au
EMAIL: info@yfc.org.au

ACKNOWLEDGEMENTS

Rod: you are the love of my life, my best friend, and confidante. I could not have written this book without your help and encouragement. You are a model of true manhood.

Adin and Lucy, Josiah and Hayley, Kezia and Elijah, Eli and Tess: my fan club who encourage me constantly and have taught me so much. I remain always your Mama Bear.

Mum and Dad: I have so much gratitude. Thank you for your perseverance in demonstrating your incredible faith in good times and bad, you are honoured.

My YFC family: it's been such a fun journey! I'm continually inspired and challenged by your overflowing joy and passion.

To those who shared their stories with me throughout this book: my sincere gratitude, I know that your testimonies will be an inspiration to many.

Mike: for challenging me to write better and with more clarity. You are so appreciated.

Jade: you are a Godsend and have assisted me so well to see this vision to fruition.

Jesus Christ: For God so loved ... the grace that has been poured out on my life is inconceivable.

You hem me in behind and before and lay your hand upon me.

– Psalm 139:5

CAN YOU HELP?

Reviews are everything to an author because they mean a book is given more visibility. If you enjoyed this book, please review it on your favorite book review sites and tell your friends about it. Thank you!

OTHER BOOKS BY CINDY MCGARVIE

The Next Revolution: Resisting the Cult of the Self

Christians were once known for their purity, selflessness, and brotherly love, but today there is often little discernible difference between the church and the world.

In *The Next Revolution*, McGarvie explores the influences that have shaped society and crept into Christian thinking since the cultural revolutions of the '60s and '70s, exposing the deceptions of self-worship and stripping them back to their ugly foundations with clarity and wisdom.

All proceeds from the sale of this book support the work of Youth for Christ Australia—raising up the next generation of evangelists and disciples.

Available from: store.yfc.org.au

www.ingramcontent.com/pod-product-compliance
Lightning Source LLC
Chambersburg PA
CBHW070257010526
44107CB00056B/2483